Elusive peace

the mind journal of a person living with anxiety

Deepti Premsagar

BlueRose ONE.com
Stories Matter
NewDelhi • London

BLUEROSE PUBLISHERS
India | U.K.

For permissions requests or inquiries regarding this publication, please contact:

BLUEROSE PUBLISHERS
www.BlueRoseONE.com
info@bluerosepublishers.com
+91 8882 898 898
+4407342408967

ISBN: 978-93-7542-134-4

Cover design: Rohit
Typesetting: Namrata Saini

First Edition: December 2025

Special Dedication

To my mother for being my guardian angel, a miraculous guiding force, spirit of positivity, my pillar of strength, my light of wisdom. To her unconditional love and support and fierce protection, I owe her my life. For her precious presence in my life which I can never relinquish.

Foreword

I am delighted to write this foreword to a book by Deepti, who I have known for almost 15 years. Deepti impressed me with a unique ability- an ability to reach out and trust, at the very time when every ounce of being says "hide, don't be seen, don't be heard".

I have seen her pursue the passion of seeking knowledge with academic rigour, crafting her own growth despite the challenges she faced within and without. In this book, she brings together lived experience with science and evidence, presenting an excellent read that does not paint a false bed of roses but a true sense of hope. I commend this book to the reader.

Dr Jairam Kamala Ramakrishnan

FRCPsych, FRANZCP, MPH, Consultant Psychiatrist

(Honorary Senior Lecturer in Psychological Medicine, University of Auckland, New Zealand

Honorary Consultant in Public Health & Liaison Psychiatry, Institute of Palliative Medicine, India)

Dedication

To my baby, Mairav for being my miracle, my joy, and my reason to live. My husband, Prem for his sacred presence in my life. To my guide and mentor, Dr. Jairam for his valuable time in writing the foreword. It is truly a blessing to receive the insights of someone of his order

My parents for being my source, my pillars, my strength, and the wind beneath my wings. My extended family for their loving support.

To God, for everything.

Contents

1. Mirages of Peace

Anxiety has the inordinate ability to make peace feel elusive and unattainable. It is one of the most complex tussles of the mind and seems impossible to resolve. For a person living with anxiety and depression, peace is a mirage that is often distant and a lasting farce. Anxiety tells the most convincing falsities about life and one's decisions. What is most challenging is to gain the ability to discern the difference between truth and falsity and gain clarity to traverse through life.

For me, experientially, life has thrown complex challenges in this respect. There are instances of blurring of truth making it impossible to gain the necessary clarity. Anxiety and depression plague the mind in ways that seem unimaginable and complex. Such is the complexity of the mind's struggle to attain the mirages of peace. It becomes impossible to decipher the truthful intent of the mind's picturization of events as most of life feels rushed and panic-laden. They are brushed in with anxious thoughts that hold testimony to transferring truth in small vials with impeccable fragility.

When one is breakable and fragile, the mind plays games that orient one's cognition toward believing the catastrophic barrage of ideas that is ushered in a flight. They are impossible to dismiss due to the conviction of their purpose. They have the ultimate purpose of enforcing the belief of intense emotions that accompany these moments of panic. Traces of mind's logic are seen in moments of relief that appear temporarily in instances where peace evades the constant companion of anxiety.

Understanding anxiety:

The American Psychological association (APA) defines anxiety as *"An emotion characterized by apprehension and somatic symptoms of tension in which an individual anticipates impending danger, catastrophe, or misfortune"* (American Psychological Association). This definition, in itself characterises the empty and distraught feelings of guilt, overwhelm, helplessness accompanied by the barrage of numerous catastrophic thoughts. The emotions of overwhelm push one to believe that each day of life is a battle to survive. Such survival instinct and the feeling of "braving" through everyday life makes it difficult to distinguish real danger from perceived danger.

Anxious thoughts form a preoccupation in the restless mind that draw gratification from starting off false signals of danger causing the mind to race in unprecedented panic. Such episodes can last all day and sometimes shorter durations depending upon the intensity of the episode. These panic-ridden thoughts have the ability to convince the mind that all sorts of unimaginable dangers lie right ahead, especially consuming the fear surrounding loved ones giving off the signals of danger and a calm before the storm. Depressive anxiety is persistent and lasts at the back of the mind perennially. It consumes the inner joy in ways one cannot perceive leaving one with a hollow experiential emotion. It makes lasting through the day exhausting and feeds on emotional fatigue and burnout.

Depression and Anxiety

Depression and anxiety are both like two sides of a single coin. They convert the normal routines of everyday into a strife that varies the situational complexity making regular life seem like a struggle. This, accompanied by overthinking can cause a major drift in one's ability to process the truth. I have, in experience felt hollow and burned out in times when things were going presumably well in the lens of the society in my life. All days felt incomparably long and exhausting to the mind. Emotional well-being is a goal most people set for their existential crisis without arriving at a specific method to resolve the panic and anxiety.

Anxiety in women

The statistics is, perhaps, alarming. Women, especially suffer from generalised anxiety disorder (GAD) and it is considered the second most frequent disorder in a primary care setting following depression (Maier et al, 2000; Uriel Halbreich, 2003). The odds ratio of women to men has been reported as being 2.2 (Wittchen and Hoyer, 2001).

Women face the ruins of the mind with grace, they say. Does the chaos in their minds revel in the whirlwinds created by the patterns of self-destruction? Slowly but surely women tend to face the wrath of the society in their stride ingesting the venomous taunts of image destruction, character assassination, dismissal, and several more rungs of the same ladder. The blunting of self-esteem is a real phenomenon. It has wings that seem tied to the joist of heavy poles that convince the mind that it cannot fly.

The role of the endocrine system:

The endocrine system has a considerable role in the development of anxiety and depression in women. The hormones such as oestrogen, progesterone, and traces of testosterone present in women influence the mental health in women. These hormones fall out of balance they lead to issues in mental health (Female Hormones and Mental Health).

The stress hormone, cortisol, affects the mental health of women to a large extent. The drop in the levels due to several physiological reasons can lead to anger, resentment, and anxiety in women. High levels of stress can cause increase in cortisol leading to physiological symptoms such as obesity and digestive disorders. Mental health issues like depressive anxiety are aftermaths of these hormonal changes.

In the life cycle of women, there are several hormonal changes that occur through puberty, menstrual cycles, pregnancy, postpartum, and menopause.

The changes in endocrinal secretions i.e. hormones lead to variations in insulin and blood sugar levels. These changes further reduce the level of serotonin, the happiness hormone. Women, since ages are left to feel like a burden. Their mental health remains to be assembled and joined back together like shards – with sharp edges. They not only cut through the flesh – they live with you as constant reminders of seething pain and fear that are seldom well-founded. I have experiential basis to say that these create a sense of gripping fear that seem unsurmountable and real. Life feels like a constant battlefield to brave through. Every social interaction is a farce and an ordeal that needs to be ticked off the dreaded check list. Where does one find her voice whilst dripping in fear hanging on to a minute speck of hope that sparkles with a dazzling, almost brazen light.

My journey:

Childhood: throughout my childhood, I remember being in two distinct phases: either as neglected as the furniture in the room or ridiculed like a peculiar animal. The word "peculiar" strikes me with distinct pain as it was used to mock me throughout my days of school. I was called 'peculiar witch' for being the quietest girl around. I was mocked for every single element of my being. I was made to feel absurd in the most hurtful ways.

Depression sets in like slow rays of moonlight, grasping the being in its fake-nice embrace. Its warmth is welcoming and may be confused for dull sunshine. You feel like living there in the space of self-pity foreshadowed by peaceful lived experiences. You do not want to face the cruel world. It is too much for you and introversion has its warm fingers wrapped around your cold and lonely mind. It is most welcoming and can pull one towards itself with all its might.

I was falsely accused of stealing a book and had no voice to defend myself. I was falsely blamed and targeted, still lacking the voice to speak out. I was never given the opportunity to defend myself and whenever I was, I did not find my voice.

Work life

I chose careers where I could sit in my cocoon and closed cabin and work like a recluse. I wanted no consultation with anybody else. I wanted to retire into spaces where I could be invisible, but industrious. I thrived in jobs involving intense academic research and writing, editing etc. I could do all of this alone and then wish for written feedback. I was appalled at the thought of attending meetings and zoom calls with the video on option. I was an incorrigible introvert throughout my life. I filled my cabin and table with idols of gods who spoke to me and held me in their warm, white embrace. I wished for sunrays, the first rays of dawn to soothingly hold me close through my God who looked upon me with His protective aura.

Pregnancy and anxiety:

Through my personal lived experience, I remember the jolt of panic spreading its black claws and seeping in like dark venom in every vein of my body during pregnancy. The sudden upsurge in the episodes of panic was unreal. It caused deafening shrieks of fear in my ever-trembling heart where peace seemed too far-fetched.

Through every journey in the car, my mind raced to the speeding (perceived) vehicles, the sound of the horn blaring in my ear causing me to cry in stifles hoping for the ordeal to end.

Every trip to the hospital felt like a battle with building rage about the driver (most often my husband or father) about their 'speeding' and seemingly inconsiderate ways of ignoring my yelling heart. My mind seemed to beg them to stop, perceiving catastrophic ideas of the car crashing, my losing my baby at every jump on the speed breaker, raging at the person sounding the horn, the sea of vehicles competing to speed. My heart was pounding imagining the end of the world and how so many people would simply end each other's lives through sheer inconsideration and lack of civility. These catastrophes played out in my mind like rushes of cinema – completely rushed.

My heart begged for peace and silence often rushing home and locking myself in my room – to breathe. These breathers kept me alive. The panic was undeniably high as it left no traces of life within me. The excitement of having my baby in my arms was doused with the fear of exposing him to the harsh world. Harsh as it seemed to me – I could only look at rough edges all cluttering into one and glaring down upon me.

Research says that pregnancy affects women' s mental health considerably. During the gestation and postpartum. The changes in the levels of oestrogen and progesterone affect the neurotransmitters like serotonin and GABA, often stunting them leading to stress reactions.

Antidepressant Usage in Pregnancy 1976 - 2008

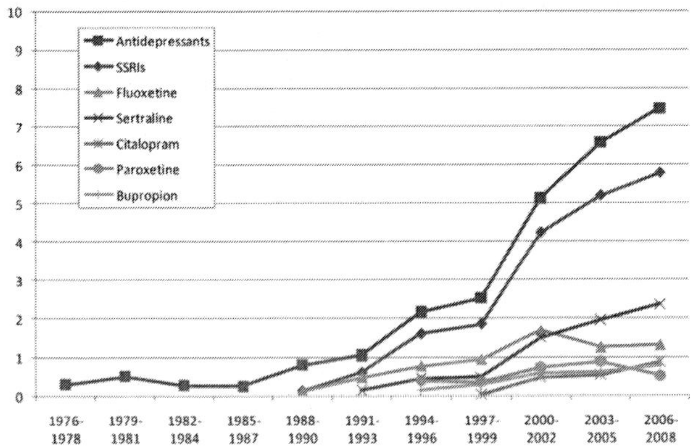

Source: A. Mitchell, et al. "Medication use during pregnancy, with particular focus on prescription drugs: 1976-2008. *Am J Obstet Gynecol* (2011) 205:E1-51.

The figure shows the usage of antidepressants in pregnancy that reaches a high. This indicates the increase in the level of anxiety and depression in women during pregnancy.

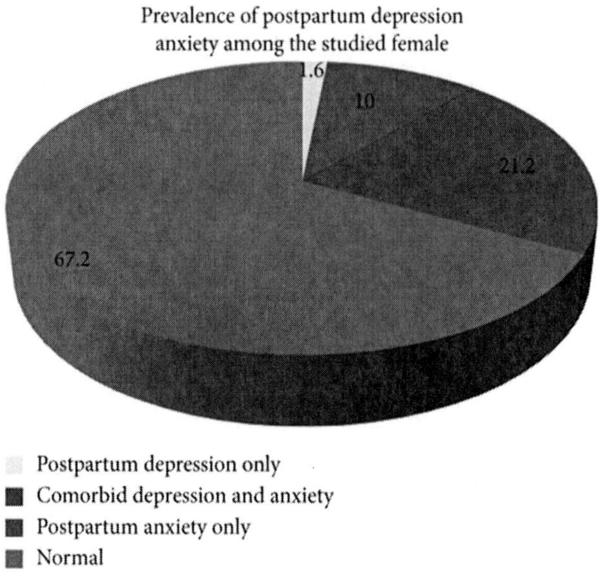

The above figure shows the statistics of anxiety and depression in women in the postpartum period. It shows the prevalence of depression and anxiety in women in the postpartum phase which takes a long time to recover from. It is a long-lasting comorbidity that one never gets used to living with.

Mirages of peace:

Peace comes in mirages that fleet past the mind like promising oases that seem ever-lasting. One looks for permanence in these fleeting moments. It is of very little consequence how this peace is attended and one feels normal – like a normal individual. That is all I crave – feeling normal. No anxiety and panic. Just normal. However, these moments are ever so fleeting that they do not even leave a trace of once having been present.

They drift away so quickly, and often reduce me to tears like that is my only identity. Peace is conditional and comes with preludes that are often hard to fulfil. It stays as long as it minds and slowly drifts away too far-fetched to muster.

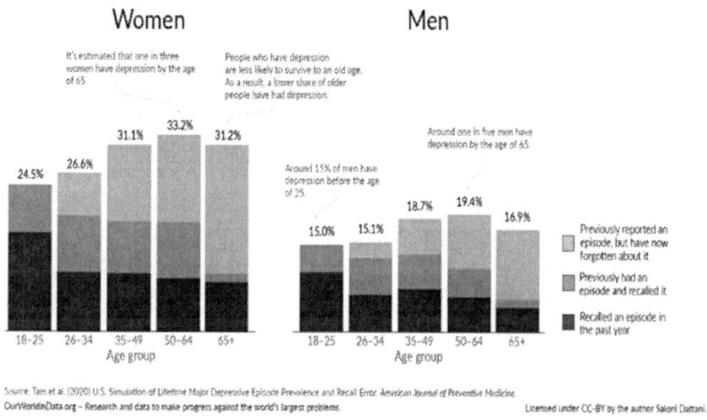

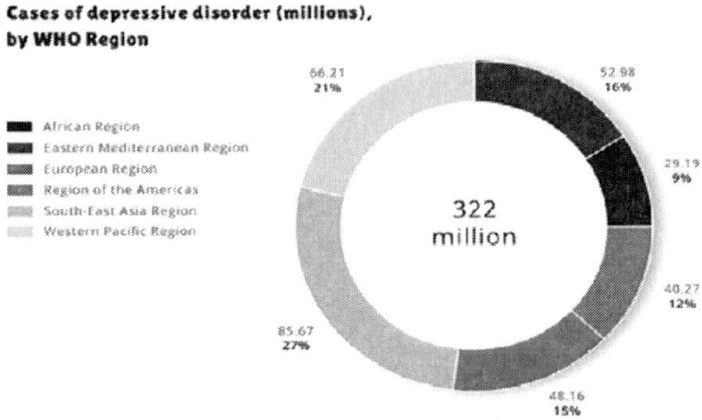

Source: lovecurelife.com

The cases of depression and anxiety in women are alarmingly high. These are not just restricted to women. Adults in general face anxiety and depression a great deal as revealed by the statistics. They fail to muster the courage to remain as strong individuals and often succumb to it. The rates of suicide are also high in adults who frequently deal with depressive anxiety. It is often endogenous and does not scream for attention. Only in moments of isolation, it slowing spreads its arms in stifling grasp, making it hard to breathe.

Anxiety is an experience that places enormous pressure on the individual. I have experienced its piercing pain in my heart since I was a child. Unknowingly, still, what anxiety truly means. Most often, anxiety is accompanied by depression. Depression of the endogenous kind. It coexists with the mind, convincing one that it is all there is to the mind. It makes up for the mind's voice. It is a part of you – inseparable as breath. Breathing and anxious thoughts go together and they form a cascade. They are your life cells and they are all you have. They make up for the most of one's thoughts – I believe all. They further push one away from truth and tell lies of the most atrocious kind. It is essential to keep one's thoughts together as they scatter themselves in all places like a burr of a tenacious plant. They colour the sky yellow – a shade of waiting, where you can neither go nor stay.

2. Anxiety and Tranquil Moments

Tranquility

Tranquillity comes in moments that are transient and often thought-provoking. They are such life-changing moments that they feel unreal and heavy. They leave me with a heavy heart and yearning for them. They stay in cosy corners and places I cannot live in. They stay in hospital feeding rooms with cosy sofas and curtains, they stay in moments of eating toasted bread and sipping warm coffee with my mother, they stay in the tips of fingers as she oils my hair, they stay in warm bites of night's supper like shreds of simple existence.

I have often attained tranquillity but it has slipped away through my anxious hands struggling to hold on to it. It has come like droplets of rain that have startled me and soothed me at once.

Tranquil moments arrive at times one least expects them to. They are vials of fulfilment and embody a quiet strength that fills the heart with hope for the next days. However, life goes on to remind you that these are not everlasting. They are transient and shall pass too quickly away, slipping away from any iron grip. It is worthy of mention that life is shrouded in the mystery of not knowing what is next. The transience of these moments is both heart-rending and alarming.

The disease biology of anxiety

Anxiety is a disorder. We have established that. Let us now delve deeper into the neuropsychological mechanism of anxiety. The septo-hippocampal system is involved in the mechanism of development of anxiety. The main difference between fear and anxiety is that in anxiety the predator's presence is only potential. There is both active and passive avoidance. This can be called the 'defensive direction'. The analysis of fear and anxiety occurs with a smoothly guided defensive distance (Gray & McNaughton, 2024). Anxiety is an experiential state. The most direct objective measure of this state is the human observer. The most practical way is the neural control of anxious behaviour. This can be ascertained through neuroimaging techniques in animal subjects that reveal the neurological pattern of thinking with anxiety. The gap between the human reports of anxiety and animal brain systems needs to be bridged (Gray & McNaughton, 2024).

There have been several starting points to this research. The most direct one is the electrical stimulation of the brain to elicit the different types of defensive behavioural patterns. The 'flight' behaviour or escapism or 'fight', the defensive behaviour can be elicited as proven in long-standing research. This can be carried out through the stimulation of medical hypothalamus and central periaqueductal grey. In majority of the instances, the parameters of stimulation determine the response to be elicited. The 'flight-fight' mechanism is a unified system delineating this response with an important role of the environment and atmosphere of the study (Gray & McNaughton, 2024).

The second starting point is the amygdalocentric orthodoxy, the point of anxious development. The neural stimulus is paired as a conditional and unconditional stimulus eliciting a variety of conditioned responses. These tend to be interpreted as fear. This fear is conditioned. The initial neural stimulus such as a flash of light or a brief tone is paired into the Pavlovian conditioning paradigm as a conditioned and unconditioned stimulus (Gray & McNaughton, 2024). The responses are perceived as fear increased heart rate, freezing or immobilisation etc are signs that are often interpreted as fear signals. However, conditioned fear is not equal to human anxiety and it is more closely related to phobia (Gray & McNaughton, 2024).

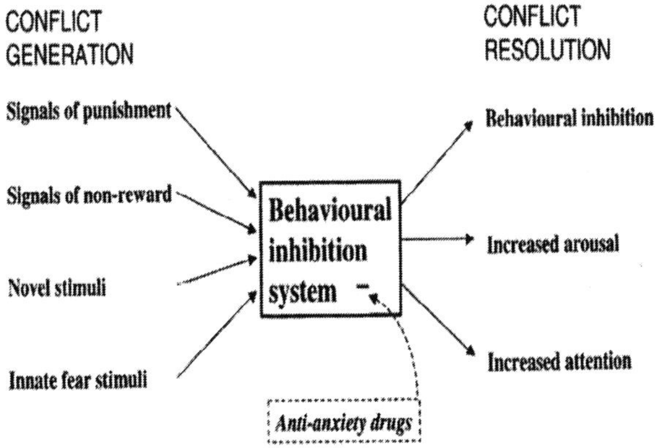

Figure: The behavioural inhibition system (Gray 1982). The inputs are CONFLICT GENERATION while CONFLICT RESOLUTION indicates the outputs.
source: (Gray & McNaughton, 2024).

The third starting point lies in the behavioural effects of the anxiolytics or drugs which reduce anxiety either reported by self or assessment of the physician (Gray & McNaughton, 2024).

A fourth starting point lies in the effects of human brain lesions. In arguably extreme cases of anxiety, which is resistant to both psychological and pharmacological treatments, a degree of success has been attributed to psychosurgery or lesions of the prefrontal cortex (Gray & McNaughton, 2024).

FEAR VS ANXIETY

Fear and anxiety are clearly distinguishable entities. They are separate in mechanism as well as in purpose. The presence of the predator being actual or potential plays a crucial role in determining this difference. In research, the animal models were placed into dangerous situations and the response observed prior to placing them was anxiety. While in the section of animals that were removed from a dangerous situation, it was fear. Thus, it may be inferred that the anticipation of danger is anxiety.

Hierarchical defence system:

There is a system that surrounds the defence mechanism in the human mind. It reflects the hierarchy of the response to stimuli that generate anxiety. The figure below represents the system in the human mind. This is, technically, the seat of anxiety. The central grey and the hypothalamus, the amygdala, the septo-hippocampal system and the frontal and cingulate cortices. These are all the different inferences of the seat of anxiety. It is clear in research that each of these regions play their own role in the development of anxiety (Gray & McNaughton, 2024).

The hierarchical defence system

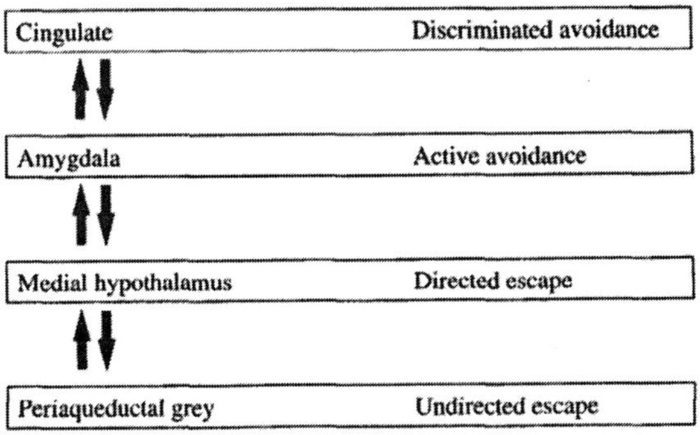

Figure: A simplified hierarchical imagery of the organisation of defence systems source: (Gray & McNaughton, 2024)

The science of anxiety reveals the depths of the neurological system that are affected by the presence of the potential perceived risk.

Birth trauma and anxiety

Psychological birth trauma is a very complex and comprehensive concept. It has previously been thought to be simpler. Birthing experiences and negative birth trauma can impact both the postpartum mental health of a woman as well as the baby (Sun et al., 2023).

I have had a complex birthing experience. There was reported suffocation due to loss of amniotic fluid and looping across the neck. It was an emergency caesarean section birth. The birth of my baby was a C-section birth with looping as well. These traumas have led to anxiety and depression perceivably (Sun et al., 2023).

I have, in times felt absolutely immobilised by thoughts of potential catastrophes, not being able to breathe normally. The wait to feel human and normal once again is endless. It is tender, fragile, and breakable. Faith can move mountains, they say. I have tried placing immense faith on rocks of discipline and God not deferring from it only to feel anxiety with more depth and pain in the depths of my heart. Only wanting to lie down and not fear that the fan may fall down upon my baby, just wishing for the boon of being able to fall asleep without the searching thoughts and memories of anxious moments is uncertain and troubling. It breaks your heart in several ways. It is impossible to understand or decipher the reason for such deafening numbness and seething pain that burns the heart, makes it run faster, makes the world seem inconsiderate and cruel, convincing the mind that death is the only respite. It is in moments of envy that I felt when those who received wishes to rest in peace that I realised the gravity of my disorder.

Waiting for life to happen

I believe I have waited for life to happen more than I have lived my life in the present. The years I have spent waiting seemed too tremendous to handle. I was a child and then a young adult and finally an adult. Through all these stages, I felt my periods of longing and waiting seemed to grow with each of them.

As a child, I was either most neglected or most bullied. I was ignored more than the furniture of the room, being absent in soul in those wretched rooms. In the classroom, I was an insignificant piece of furniture abused when one was bored. I was called the most appalling names and was beaten and bullied. My lunch box was snatched from me and its contents, thrown into the bin like trash. My heart swelled in silent tears that burnt my cheeks on their way down. In those moments of silent anguish, my thoughts wandered off to the unnecessary meanness and lack of kindness amongst my fellow children.

Just because an individual is quiet and timid, does it make way for the other individuals to bully them and treat them without humanity? The lack of humanity and civility with striking barbarism among people, especially children is alarming. It strikes one as dangerous and preposterous. The realisation that people are inhuman and inconsiderate reflects in the behaviour of children. Considering the situation was this poor in the 1990's, it must be worse in the present times, where artificial intelligence has taken over life and the human side of life is slowly disappearing. It is of surmount importance then, that one should believe in truths that cross the apparitions of brazen faces that cross the roads every single day.

My thoughts seem best expressed in the lines that I once penned out of nowhere. It is in these moments of nothingness that I pen poems that paint the hues of my heart's deepest fears, happinesses, and yearnings.

To the shadows that once fell
into the depths of the relentless ocean,
there must be hidden treasures there
where no one dares to look.
I hold those moments in silent faith
to bring the storms together
they scatter, they stray
and finally, depart.

I have delved in the most uncertain depths of truth and its namesakes. There have been multiple episodes of depression as a child where I have wondered how to set right my emotions and correct the lethargy that came with it. There was a constant need to be alone and in quiet nooks of the classroom. The unruly behaviour of other children and high noise levels bothered me more than it did the teachers.

My parents must have had expectations from me that I always strived to meet but felt like I ended up failing. I always felt a tad bit lower than their expectations. I scored well on my exams, was one of the most well-behaved children, played tennis to a considerably good level, performed Bharatnatyam to a considerable level as well. However, I never culminated any of my skills to completion. My self-talk was self-bashing and a perennial sense of shame and guilt for no apparent reason.

My childhood was spent in a race. A race to fulfil parental expectation. Comparisons with other kids broke my heart in unmendable ways. I was beyond repair as my thoughts wandered off to places that I could not reach. They were far beyond my access. These crevices of my mind were unstable and difficult to gain control of. I constantly was buried in a feeling of inferiority with the other kids. I felt like they were superior to me in unexplainable ways.

The feeling of inadequacy was haunting. It broke my heart and shattered my dreams. I was a timid child and a vulnerable teenager. I wore my heart on my sleeves. It was the most challenging task to ascertain what in me was broken and how much.

It is most important in life to know this as it is what makes life happen. I went through life in a confused cycle of never-ending depression. I felt life was complex and was afraid of my surroundings. I was intimidated by little things like standing up to ask for extra sheet on my exams or simply to answer my attendance call. I was intimidated and found it hard to talk before a group of people. These things bothered me in the most inexplicable ways. It was of a perennial kind – making its way into normal life. The normative structure of life often bothered me the most. My mind seemed further away from this truth as can be. These traces of normalcy bothered my existence. It was in these times that I often predicted the underscored depression that haunted my life.

It is crucial to remain calm and collected as we look at the wonders of life that trickle into years of investing oneself into curing depression I have often struggled with the most exhaustive ways of cultivating peace into my everyday life. It is necessary to stay within the confines of the arbitrage of meaning as it is of immense importance. It is not natural for a person living with anxiety to feel in control. It is unnatural even to feel peace temporarily. These bouts of peace come in such fragile vials that I fear them to break every once.

It is of moral conjecture now that I need to keep attaining the temporary peaceful states in order to survive. There is no more of a great demand or prayer that exceeds these states to stay with permanence in my life. When people around you promote conflict, it is most difficult to attain or even retain peace.

3. Attaining Temporary Peace

Peace is always temporary. Its presence is soothing and inviting. It seldom stays beyond a specific time, slipping away right through my hands like rainwater. It is hard to attain peace and harder to retain it. Peace is temporary and is defiant in its ways.

Lord Krishna in the Bhagavad Gita says that peace is attainable to those who can fixate their consciousness upon him. I have, for one, tried to do so in all possible means.

भोक्तारं यज्ञतपसां सर्वलोकमहेश्वरम् ।
सुहृदं सर्वभूतानां ज्ञात्वा मां शान्तिमृच्छति ॥ २९ ॥

bhoktāraṁ yajña-tapasāṁ
sarva-loka-maheśvaram
suhṛdaṁ sarva-bhūtānāṁ
jñātvā māṁ śāntim ṛcchati

Source: https://vedabase.io/en/library/bg/5/29/

This shloka translates to English somewhat like this: A person who is in complete consciousness of Krishna and knows him to be the ultimate beneficiary of all sacrifices and austerities and knows that he is the supreme Lord of all planets and demigods. The benefactor and well-wisher of all living beings attains peace from the pangs of material miseries (Bhagavad-Gītā as it is 5.29).

This knowledge, however did not bring me the ultimate peace as I did not know how to stop worrying silly about my child. My heart screamed with pangs of anxiety wishing for a relief from these anxious, racing thoughts. I did not feel free enough to reach him and attain him as I have my son's responsibility to fulfil. I still pray for his well-being and feels pangs of guilt consuming me from within as they invoke hopelessness within me.

The spiritual meaning of peace and anxiety seem unreal and closer to God. If only one could slip away into the warm embrace of God, there would be no tussle. There have been times when death has seemed so inviting as it is of immense difficulty to move on in life when all you have is anxiety and panic attacks.

These attacks come to you like strong winds. They not only sway you; they also pull you into a whirl of relentless thoughts. They are impossible to control and cause depressive thoughts repeatedly.

It is necessary to regain composure and face life. This seems like the most difficult challenge.

I have often been bullied as a child. For wanting my mother, for being quiet, for being disciplined, kind, helpful, and timid. I have been called the most miserable names and have drowned in the rough seas of profanity from my fellow students.

The personal attacks have destroyed me emotionally and made it hard for me to resolve them within myself. I used to sit in a corner in school feeling engulfed by the air in the classroom. The air is impossible to get over as it filled my heart with depressive thoughts. It is important then to understand how people understand emotions as most people tend to gravitate towards the unimportant decisions.

It is hard for people to be kind to one another, especially when they do not know the depth of another's hurt. Opposing one's thoughts and feelings in the turmoil of the heart. It is personal happiness that involves the gratitude in the purport of emoluments that resolve their own intentions. It is ultimate importance that unless people look into the wings of one's thoughts and emotions.

I have burned in the hellfire of people's boring eyes and taunts that seer through the heart. My mind has been full of insensitive words that pour into my heart. It is full of harsh words that the world fills into the heart of a person with anxiety. It is an essential element in the nature of an anxious person to gorge on the same bittersweet thoughts.

Philosophy preaches that emotions are supposed to be under control. It is essential to gain peace through emotional stability. It is impossible to gain control over emotions that are a case in point for the unfulfilled emotions. It is a turbidity that ruins the shreds of faith that endure the strain.

Usurping the policy of peaceful truth, anxiety lies time and again telling one that the world is too harsh for the anxious. People live by feeding upon the interests of the anxious person. They target their living word of faith that endures in strain. It is this strained word of faith that pulls along in life's remotest lines. It becomes difficult to hold onto the faith and positivity that is the result of endless battles in the mind.

The mind tussles with enduring imprints that ply through the struggles of every day life. The strife is never-ending. It is a newness and rebirth every fraction of a second as the mind battles to keep up the sanity and forget hurtful remarks passed at you. I have dealt with the most profane and inhuman remarks aimed at my very existence. They have pierced into my soul and made my heart a miserable place. It is often true that people do not regard the seamless emotions that block the mental existence of an individual.

It is highly remarkable that the mind grapples with the negativity that the world spews in this direction. It is necessary to evolve and become a higher individual by addressing these changes in one's personality. It is an unusual demand of the world that people with anxiety do not regard the world as home but are expected to face the truth unflinchingly. It is such a necessity that it becomes the instability of the mind. Mind temporarily goes into spaces of negativity that spills outside the mind. Mindful execution is a response to the timely stimuli that retract in the space of time.

Lived experiences are real-time processes that gather around one's own self-respect. Those events shape the thoughts on an individual in the anxious space of life. The heart yearns for moments of peace that and the upliftment of the mind. The heart does not consent the various atrocities that fill in the mind. They hold up the natural response of the heart making it difficult to process the dissent of the world.

It is a majority of thoughts that score the yellowed pages of past days' books and looking through the skims of light that pose their inevitable energy. I have lived my life through the most silent chaos and tempests that arose in my heart. I haven't been able to I live my life with complete, unabashed confidence. It is of ultimate necessity to be in a position of confidence and strife where one can easily sail through the hardships that pose themselves. I have dealt with people who seem to enjoy the prospect of my having anxiety. It is often a topic of fun and is discussed in the lighter vein. But as a person living with anxiety, the most common moments of life like sitting in the cafeteria, working at my desk, group meetings, facing the crowd, driving back from work all of these everyday events felt big and churned the emotions of my heart making me scramble for peace. I would go up to the restroom and breathe 10 times before coming out to face the world again.

These big moments of simply existing through life felt like a challenge and made me feel like I was braving through life. The office space felt alien and sometimes most peaceful. The paradox of these things was almost parallel to regular life.

I loved going to office by 7:30 and soak in the quietness of the place. I would play devotional songs all the way to work and pull into the garage, go up to my desk, put down my bag and pour myself a cup of coffee. The moments of being alone at work were simply refreshing and wonderful. I loved being in the office at early hours and loved soaking in the freshness of the morning,

I did not particularly enjoy the time when people started trickling in and piercing into the silence of the floor with their loud, sharp voices. I was appalled at their existence and wished to be left alone. I remember feeling like I was the butt of the joke every time somebody laughed. I was convinced that they were mocking me and laughing at me.

I felt paranoid at work when I felt like people were all aiming to humiliate me. I felt like I was the target of all their mockery. My confidence fell to the ground and I was unable to pick it up. I felt like everybody around was talking ill about me for no apparent reason. These feelings were overwhelming and they overpowered my judgement. It was in these moments that I felt most lonely and like my life was a dry, barren land.

In all these times, I yearned for a companion who would understand me and my big feelings. I wished for a friend, philosopher, guide, and life partner who would be with me and tell that it was alright to feel the way I was feeling. My heart yearned for these emotions and the want of a partner was very overpowering.

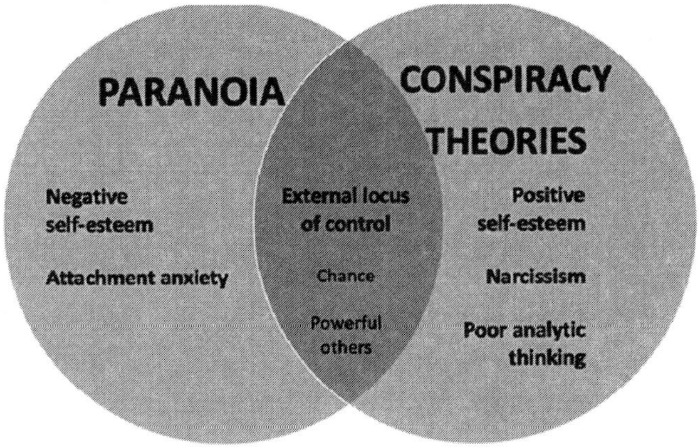

Fig: Paranoia and anxious thoughts

CITATION: Alsuhibani et al, 2022

Paranoia is an intersection with anxious thoughts and imageries. There are paranoid thoughts that intertwine with these anxieties. Negative self-esteem and the lack of positive self-image drives the person to an edge. I have often felt most challenged in these cases. The paranoia of these emotions is often overwhelming and engulfs it in its own race. I have been taken into these thoughts and had my heart full of confusing emotions and thoughts. I have often felt disturbed by these negative emotions and panic attacks that make one feel surpassed into imagination.

Eating disorder

In my experience, eating disorder had become a common outcome of anxiety. I had emotional eating and craved junk food very often. My health went down a downward spiral and I was always addicted to eating at specific joints. My pulse was always high and I never had the time to look into my heart's desires.

Every day after work, I felt overwhelmed that I had to deal with so many people. I was challenged and felt very weak and exhausted on an emotional level. Thus, I would often wish to eat at specific joints with my mother who was my only friend. I used to call her every day after work, meet her midway and eat at these places before going home. I would starve myself the entire day just to eat out at the end of the day.

Digestion issues

I have had digestion issues and diarrhoea as part of my life. I have dealt with immense issues in digestion and met with multiple doctors to resolve my issue. However, it was never a clinical or physiological problem.

Digestion issues are a common feature of anxiety and panic. The eating disorder is a common side effect of unmanaged anxiety and panic. Every panic attack was followed by junk eating. These were followed by episodes of indigestion and diarrhoea.

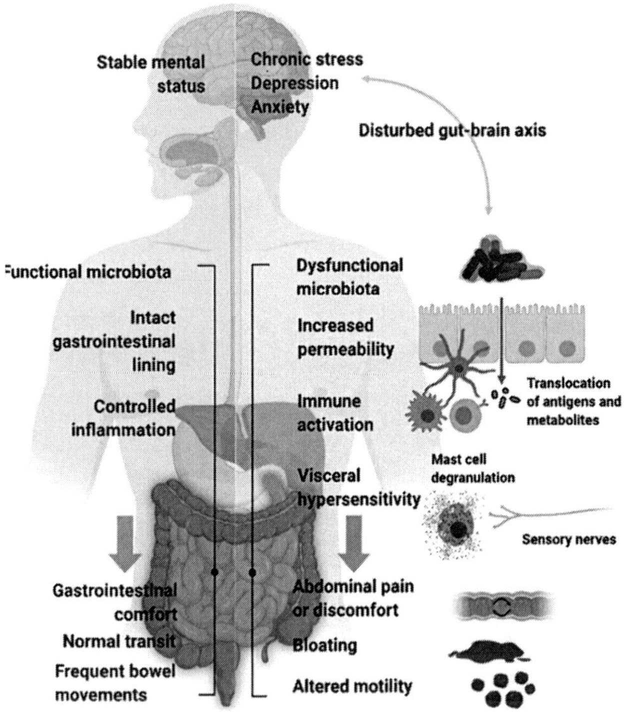

Fig. Digestive issues in anxiety
Citation: Carco Caterina et al, 2020

The figure above shows the effect of anxiety on digestion.

The human gastrointestinal tract is home to a majority of bacterial cells which form a part of the human body. There are several bacterial strains that keep the gut healthy. They have several implications on the maintenance of structural integrity of the gastrointestinal mucosal barrier, immunomodulation, metabolism of nutrients, and protection against pathogens (Carco et al, 2020). The nutrients essential for the body are often processed by food that is consumed. However, the every day food needs to be disciplined and healthy. I have, at most times, fallen prey to eating junk and processed food without a control of the mind.

Despite knowing its ill effects, I have felt compelled to break my diet and anxiously eat unhealthy food. It was an uncontrollable urge. I felt pressurised into fitting into the beauty standards of the society in order to be "selected" for marriage by suitors. I felt appalled, disgusted, and enraged at such ideas. However, I felt as further away from such beauty standards as can be. I felt I could never reach up to those standards and felt like a constant let down for my parents. I felt like I was a disaster in all.

These weak moments gave me the sole option for solace in burying my sorrows and anxieties in food. I felt I could not give up the only pleasure that I had within me. I faced several digestive issues and had the eating disorder of starving for hours and even days and then binge eating unhealthy food.

Research says that dysfunctions in these mechanisms are linked to a range of conditions in the gastrointestinal tract, including functional gastrointestinal disorders, ranging from irritable bowel syndrome, to functional constipation and functional diarrhoea (Carco et al, 2020).

I have been diagnosed with irritable bowel syndrome. Irritable bowel syndrome is characterized by chronic abdominal pain with changes in bowel habit in the absence of morphological changes. Despite the high prevalence of irritable bowel syndrome in the global population, the mechanisms responsible for this condition are poorly understood (Carco et al, 2020).

I have been in the position of not having any idea of how to navigate my emotions and how to handle them efficiently. I have had a case in point of finding my lost soul among these beastly anxious thoughts. Irritable bowel syndrome is most disturbing and a disadvantage for living.

Thus, it is important for an individual living with anxiety to control eating and lifestyle. It is crucial for us to live in braces and under the strict mindfulness of seeking peace. The stakes for living for a person with anxiety are usually high. It is important for life to be under a causal control in a lifeless tussle that concerns the imaginary boundaries that tie us up and make us go in circles.

It is an inevitable journey of living under these stressors and control the urge for eating disorder.

Studies suggest that although there are alterations in the gastrointestinal microbiota, low-grade inflammation and immune activation have been found to be implicated in the pathophysiology of functional gastrointestinal disorders, there is an observed inconsistency between studies. There is also a lack of consensus on the role of the microbes along with the changes under these conditions.

There is a complex interplay between host factors, such as microbial dysbiosis, immune activation, impaired epithelial barrier function and motility, and environmental factors, including diet, will be considered in this narrative review of the pathophysiology of functional gastrointestinal disorders.

This complex interplay is what affects the lifestyle of the persons with anxiety. It is essential to keep a tab on the food that is consumed. I have struggled to keep myself under control and keep a tab on my emotions. I have experienced a sense of loss and found myself through eating.

The eating disorder has taken a toll on me and I have failed to be in a position to control the urge to eat. I have experienced gastrointestinal infection and feared the onset of ulcers as well. I had to take medication to control the gastrointestinal regurgitation and heart burn that resulted from my eating disorder and extended starvation. There was no middle route and it was always an operation that occurred in extremes. It is essential to make a way for the enteric possibilities to develop into something large.

My mind has been going in circles and there was always a dearth for the logical understanding. I have never understood the depths of my imagination which swung both ways into the upheaval of privacy. What is the actual notion that keeps one alive?

It is a crucial task to decipher what it actually takes to make one understand the circumstantial level of existing and making peace with the living conditions. It becomes almost impossible to regain the consciousness about forming the elective of choice about how to live without anxiety. These moments of peace and stability are ever so transient. They flit away in seconds and do not gravitate or stay.

It is the underlying issue that matters the most as it is important to control the emotions that forge their way into my heart and tally with the undertaking with of rough use. It is such an anguish to keep the emotions at bay and work their way into the myriad ways of the mind.

It is an essential to make the most of such times when the mind is under control and be able to surpass the emotional level of dearness that takes away from the truth of life. It is the untruths that delve into the mind's complexes and trigger the attacks.

The panic attacks occur frequently dispute the situation and feed on the anxious repertoire of thoughts that mend their ways into inexhaustible beings. The figure below explains the trigger and the thoughts of anxiety that develop into several modes of struggle.

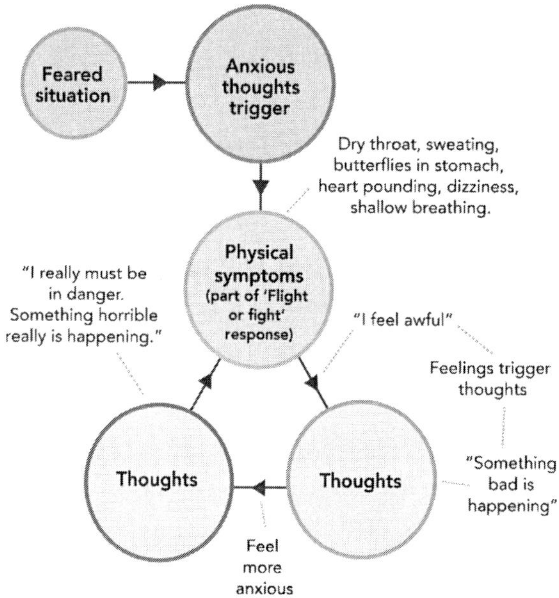

Source: https://www.mindwell-leeds.org.uk/

The above figure is a situational chart of various actions and reactions that involve in the well-being of mind feeding to situational anxiety. The flow of thoughts and anxious feelings incur the wrath of the mind. The intensity of anxiety increases with every thought.

The mind repeats the thoughts of anxiety and trigger emotional responses along with physical implications every time the feared situation comes in the purview. The fight or flight response is triggered every time the feared situation comes to the fore. The various thoughts that occur due to the perceived danger giving way to the feelings of awfulness and fear of danger.

The thoughts that occur when the feared situation comes into view are the awful feelings of a potential catastrophe. The feeling that something bad or awful is about to occur leads to physical implications such as dizziness, pounding of the heart, butterflies in the stomach etc. All these thoughts of danger occur simultaneously with the physical and emotional implications as they validate the potentiality of selfless emotions.

These often trigger the reviews of the mind that juggle between the resourcefulness of horrible acts occurring at the level of anxiety. The mind convinces self that something terrible and of great intensity is occurring.

This unpleasant feeling leads to taking precautionary actions and avoidance of the feared situation. Safety behaviors are those that help in making one feel more peaceful and to look for ways to reduce anxious thoughts. This is the automatic response of the mind where it tries to avoid the situation that causes stress.

It is the emotional response that causes the flutter of thoughts and the exhilarated feeling of wishing to escape the situation. Carrying medication or sitting closer to the exit. Such behavior is called avoidance.

source: https://www.thecandidly.com/

The above picture suggests that intrusive thoughts trigger responses that occur in the body. The medications that help in the process are prescribed by doctors to control the emotional disruption.

Intrusive thoughts occur very frequently and attack one when alone and also when in crowded spaces. The space between these thoughts is very short and the duration longer than ever. It is hard to decipher the intent of these thoughts as they do not have rationality. They cause extreme distress and do not make complete sense.

These irrational fears cannot be done away with and are all-engulfing. I have tried my best to not entertain such thoughts and tried to force pleasant thoughts into my mind. However, that strategy has failed me miserably. It is important to allow those emotions to sit and focus on them to logically defeat them. It is an impossible possibility to interlude these thoughts with positive ones and be able to replace them.

I have tried to decipher these thoughts and make the most of them to be able to understand the depth of my feelings. However, it is not a possibility to retain the peace and delineate the difference between the reality and anxious thoughts.

I have found engagement with those thoughts and have not been able to pull myself away from them. The expectation that these thoughts will come anyway remains with one. It is impossible to push them away and they demand indulgence.

I have struggled with the corners of my mind, delving deep into the possibilities and threats of the social and cognitive drama.

Significantly it is even more persistent in the mind that flows in anxious thoughts. It varies in the perspectives of those who delve into anxiety and surf its depths. Those thoughts fight for attention and they insist upon being heard.

Ruggedly, the world operates in its own chaos. It makes the wisdom of one's peaceful states undecipherable and ugly. It is with these transitions of the mind that it becomes impossible to portray the viscous emotions that infiltrate the mind.

The uncertainty that fades within the depth of one's heart makes it unclear and immersive in itself. It is justification of truth that revolves around the mental state that holds it all together.

4. The Tussle of Retaining Peace

Peace can be attained but retaining it – is the real question. It has been extremely difficult for me to retain the peace within myself as it is difficult to hold on to life's meaning in traces of peace. Peace does not stay long enough for the functionality of life. It drifts away in slow torrents like gusts of wind. Vulnerability and fragility of the mind can dictate the extent to which the human mind can function as it is hard to retain.

The tussle is infinite as peace does not remain in the folds of the arm. It takes a great effort to build it and soon withers away. Attaining this elusive peace is truly a challenge. As the Gita says, conditioned souls within the clutches of the illusory energy are all anxious to attain peace while traversing in the material world (Bhagavad-Gītā as it is 5.29). Lord Krishna says that he is the main beneficiary of all the sacrifices and worship. He indicates that by offering obeisances to Him and knowing Him as the supreme Lord who is the benefactor and the giver of faith can help one attain peace.

I am testament to this fact as I have, indeed, attained peace. However, what I have struggled with is to retain it. It is almost impossible to retain peace as it feels like a constant struggle and is inevitable in nature as one cannot hold onto the peace that is attained. Chanting and understanding God's presence does fulfil the nexus of positive thoughts flowing into the mind. However, they drift away as suddenly as they arrive.

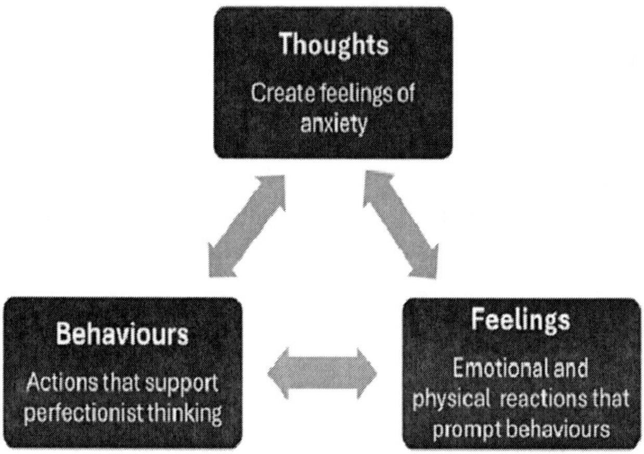

source: www.youngminds.org.uk

Peace is hard to retain as it leaves before one can even realize that it was a member of the mind. It leaves no traces in the life of those who suffer from anxiety. Behaviors and actions reflect the purpose of the mind as it sticks to gaining clarity and being able to decipher the real reason for the emptiness that it feels.

It is the most wonderful challenge to be able to retain such peace that is but elusive and transient in its very nature. The anxious thoughts cause anxious feelings and behaviours that reflect the same thought process.

Anxiety has torn in bits and pieces and worked on the shards of its ruthless knife-like edges. I had developed certain strategies to cope and turned deeply to religious media to alleviate my symptoms.

Several actions are perpetuated in emotional and physical reactions to stimuli that prompt the behavioral implications that refract the changes in the surroundings and triggering situations.

Emotional triggers can be mindlessly ruthless and can retract the solutions and that implicate the problems of the mind. These problems and situations seem terribly indispensable and one learns to live with them.

The gratitude of life and happiness about the suffused happenings indulge in truth and bravado.

The cycle of anxiety includes a behavioral model that includes a stimulus of fear that includes intrusive thoughts that deeply trigger the anxious responses. These are reinforced by the absence of correction and corrective experiences.

The corrective experience, when lacking, includes never-ending thoughts that are okay and can be handed without behaviors of safety.

The mind does not ever learn that these situations are temporary and free of danger and do not allow the learning behavior that reinforces the belief that the situation can be handled and it is not dangerous.

The reinforced pattern ascertains that there is absence of relief. Sometimes, corrective behavior brings about temporary relief from anxiety. Threats are misinterpreted and the presence of thoughts and sensations perceive situations as being dangerous.

The anxious mind convinces one that the situation is just not right and there is something truly wrong with the circumstance. However, the mind fails to cope with the reality that the situation is only ordinary and does not involve danger.

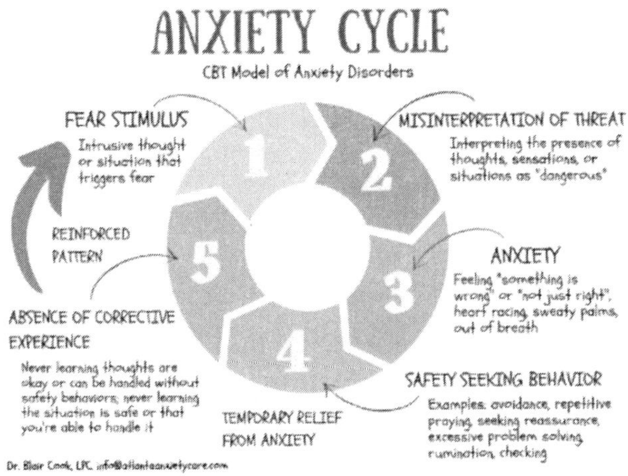

Citation: https://atlantaanxietycare.com/anxiety-cycle

I have been stuck in these situations and felt like my life was ending in perceived danger.

Once one understands the reality of the situation, it becomes increasingly difficult to push away the thought that there is an anomaly with the mind. Thus, it is of general importance to assume that these situations are all under control.

It becomes further than impossible to redeem such confidence. My mind often juggles with the innumerable ways in which ordinary situations may be turned into dangerous ones. I have most often struggled to cope with the gravity of these situational anxieties that feel so real and captivating. It is such an enhancement to the soul that life resonates its unheard truths.

In a poem I once penned, I attempted to capture this fear:

In apparitions that solidify the verdant mirage
I have learned to appreciate the little things
The twinkling stars, the shining sun, and the soft moon
Reflections of bare truth scream their existence
In futile attempts to nurture the sense
Of living life unflinchingly.

These lines showcase the confused emotions of the anxious mind.

I remember soaking the sun in summer afternoons and lying on my bed, reading religious books or chanting *mantras* also doing *suryanamaskars.* None of these helped alleviate the lump in my throat and the heap of disgust in the pit of my stomach.

I call this heartburn, sadness, lump, and heap depression. This is depression as I have known it – in its barest and most hideous form. I was never diagnosed and people told me to remain 'strong'. A word I began to despise for the sheer number of times I was told that.

I was told that I am too fragile for the world. I am too sensitive. I am too much. I believed the same narrative until my mind crushed itself in guilt for taking up just too much emotional space in the lives of my loved ones.

I started to believe in the proverbial end. I attempted to put and end to life several times and failed. However, I believe the harshest truths only nurture reality and not my futile imagination. How far does one go to attain peace?

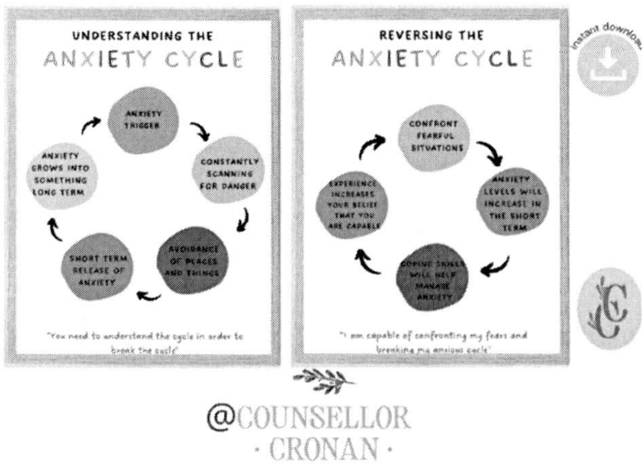

Source: https://www.artofit.org/

Understanding the truth of life is indeed an amazing task. My life has gone in circles. All the times that I have wondered if anything will change at all are enormous.

I have often sat in the coffee break at office sipping on the machine-made coffee, looking up at the empty sky, reminiscing my empty prayers. I have felt like life is a continuous and vicious loop.

I remember attempting to manifest marriage and future life in the traditional and religious setting. I remember feeling ugly and unwanted. I remember comparing myself to a puppy in a story I read as a 7-year-old. The puppy that waits endlessly in a kennel trying to mold himself into dogs that were picked each time.

The puppy that tries to be everybody but himself and attempts umpteen times to impress potential owners and trying to live up to their expectations.

I remember trying to impress potential suitors to 'pick me' for marriage. I remember trying to get married and push onto the future of my life. And failing.

The stress of wanting to become another individual and wishing to manifest liking from other individuals has been too heavy on my heart. Words that pierced through my soul told me I was never enough. They told me I was ugly and worthless.

I believed them. I believed them all. I believe I still do – believe them. It was impossible to imagine life without a companion and impossible to imagine a companion devoid of marriage. I wanted the sacred thread around my neck with the witness of the sacred fire we call '*Agni*' in our dharma.

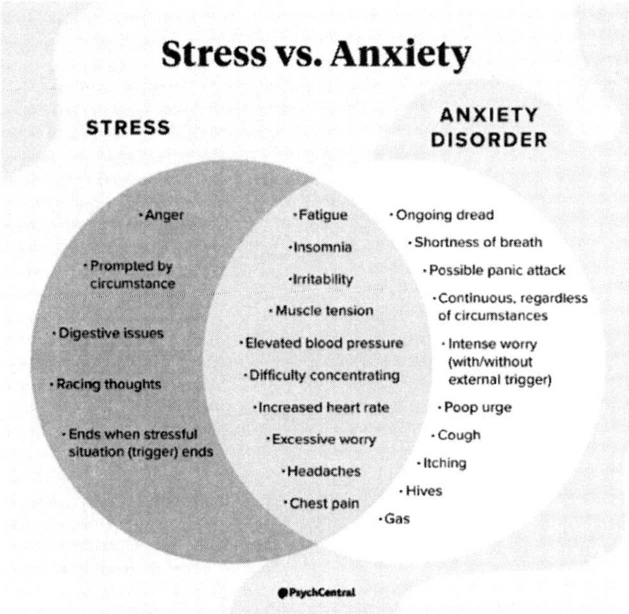

Source: https://psychcentral.com/

I have feared death as a lonely woman, a spinster and a dreaded 'crazy cat woman'. I have hated this prospect enough to decide to kill myself. I have feared dying in this state and being desperate for marriage.

I have experienced severe depression and anxiety and stress. Altogether. The situational anxiety is coupled with anger, frustration, racing thoughts, and digestive issues. These problems were resonated in my wish to travel the world to fulfill empty promises I once made – to myself.

5. Elusive Nature of Peace

The longing for calm amidst chaos is like thirst. The longing for water to the man who is thirsty. There is nothing else in the world, no matter how luxurious that can calm the thirst roused in the person who is thirsty. There is no other thought in the mind except to drink water and be able to quench that thirst. The longing for peace is such. It is not quenched by peace that comes in bubbles of water that only wet the lips and do not reach the dry and longing throat.

It simply teases the mind with its elusive presence for transitory moments before rushing away to an unknown land far away from reality. It is hard to imagine how to reach this insurmountable goal.

Peace, they say is a profound connection to one's inner self. It encompasses serenity, harmony, and completeness. It is, unlike the popular opinion, something beyond the absence of conflict. Conflict is the challenge that people with anxiety face. The prospect of conflict can even make one feel terrorized at the imaginary occurring following a showdown in the family. It is also terrorizing to have meltdowns for several reasons. My emotions have often gotten out of control and there have been times where I have been unable to understand the reasons for such meltdowns.

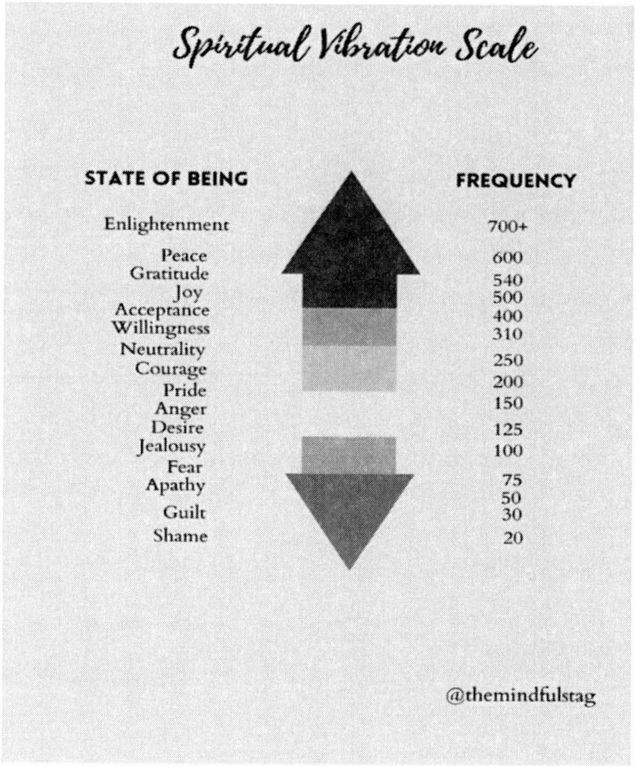

source: storage.googleapis.com

The figure above showcases the states if being on a mental level and the effects of these instances. Anxiety causes a deep emotional turmoil leading to events that not only restrict a person's functionality, they also cause one to undergo a regressive transformation in terms of social well-being.

Anxiety and depression along with all negative emotions are shown to have very low frequencies. These emotions cause a deepening of a sense of regret, resentment, anger, and frustration. These emotions largely impact the well-being and holistic mental health of an individual.

I have been influenced by these emotions to great extents and felt completely zoned out and impossibly drained in my heart. Such emotions leave a lasting impact on one's vision of life and create a chaotic mental environment.

The effort it takes to monitor such emotions and get over them is immense. It reduces the patience and ability to have a distinction between the localization of emotions as well as their globality. Thus, it becomes harder and harder to ascertain the depth of one's own feelings as they scream loudly in anguish deepening the fright that one attaches to being alive.

The negative emotions seem to invade one's territory of peace. They make their way right through the walls that one builds in vain to keep them at bay. These low-frequency of emotions drain a person's wellness and health to an unshakeable extent.

It is most frustrating to learn that these are the emotions that one struggles to ward off. The blackness of the walls that surround the mind freeze in all its glory. It is important to realize one's mettle to understand the crevices of their own mind in all its glaring complexity. It is often a maze that rushes one to make choices that fulfill these desires.

Death often feels welcoming. Its warm, dark embrace seems like the lasting light at the end of the never-ending tunnel. You wish to embrace it in all its warmth and peace. That is when one can rest in peace. The elusive, elusive peace.

I have experienced deep pain in trying to retain life's patterns that stole away from the purpose of life. Making decisions difficult and nights longer than they were supposed to be as I juggled between the positives and negatives of life's crossroads that entered and exited my judgement of peace.

I have been betrayed not once, but again and again by peace.

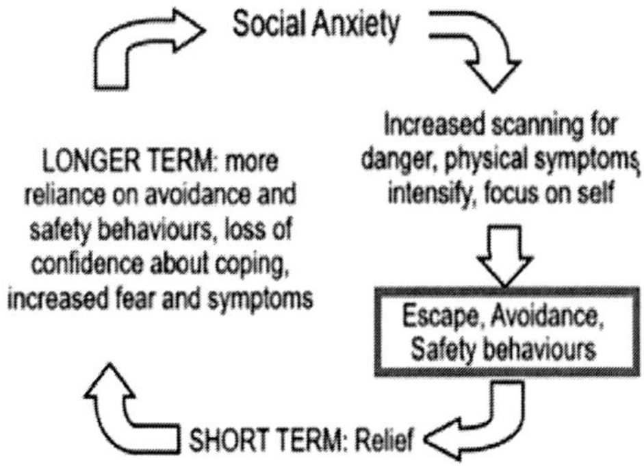

Source: https://socialanxietyalliance.org.uk/

One of the patterns of anxiety is social anxiety that manifests in the long term as avoidance of social situations. I used to feel overwhelmed and desperate for silence.

Prior to marriage, I avoided social gatherings and weddings for the fear of being asked if I was planning to get married and what plans I had for my future. However, I had no plans to reveal. I felt like bursting into tears and saying I did not see a future. I wished to say that I did not really know what I wished to do with my life.

I felt entangled in the questions that my mind started every single time. I did not have answers. I avoided social contact and meeting people.

I have been baffled by the questions thrown at me by my mind. I have felt paranoid and reluctant.

The reluctance was about the situations that people may look at and feel like I was a burden to the world.

I felt like I was an anomaly and was too ugly to be accepted for marriage. I constantly felt like I was too much and too far from 'perfection'. I was too old, too ugly, too fat, and too unfit for life.

These thoughts dominated my existence and made me feel neglected.

The response to stress in the brain is shown in the illustration. The brain perceives stress as being equivalent to physical pain. Such pain is not, in the least bit dismissible and makes waves in the mind that are hard to ignore.

My heart has yearned for peace and has wished to be desired. I have often felt like I was a burden to the universe. I have felt neglected and unseen.

Social gatherings caused immense stress. Stress to prove myself and to feel presentable. The brain has experienced painful pauses that seethed in anger and envy about women who had partners. I have felt appalled at myself for feeling these emotions.

The stress of looking composed and feeling calm was too high for existence. I have often struggled with anxiety and disorders of mood that have felt disengaged from the predicaments of facing relatives.

Mood swings are dysregulated emotions that lead to inflammation of several points of the brain leading to physical pain.

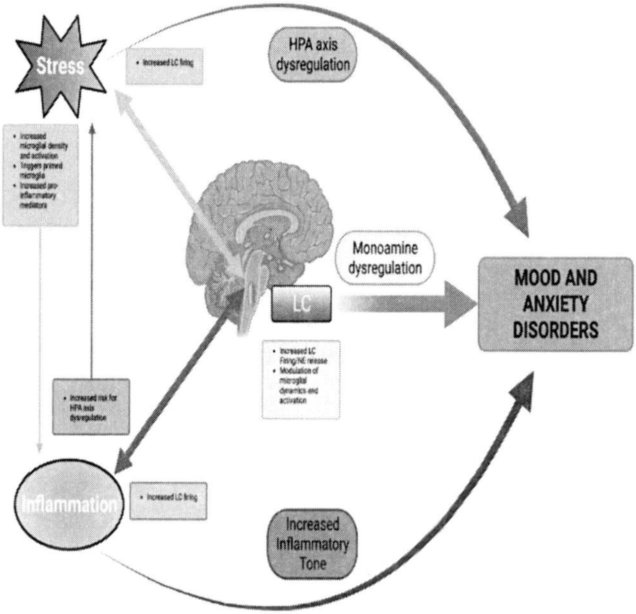

Source: https://www.mdpi.com/

The physical pain feels unreal and dramatic and too hard to control. They are often coupled with useless stressors of life that seem to tell you untruths that are hard to ignore.

6. Diagnosis and Treatment

Diagnosis is validation, while treatment is conditional relief. It is the first step to understanding the clinical implications of the condition and its neurological pathology and disease biology. It provides self-compassion and releases the pressing guilt.

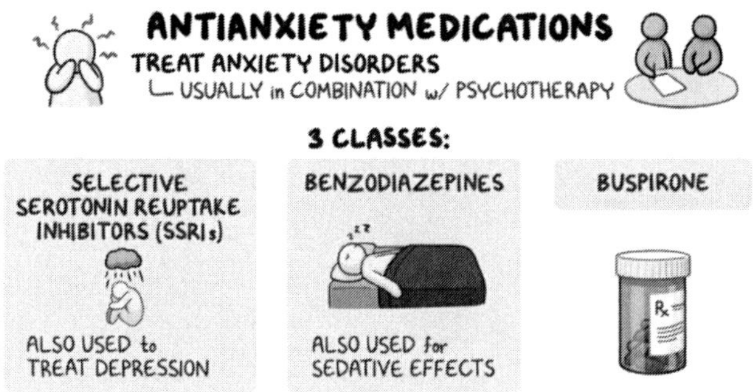

source: www.osmosis.org

Diagnosis is the validation that results in a sense of satisfaction as the doctor is able to understand the big and difficult emotions that one feels. It is the finding of peace in such voluntary validations that make it all the more worth it.

It is the most challenging to understand how to work your way around the emotions you so deeply feel.

It is such enhancement of the emotion that makes it all the more challenging. I have experienced a deep-set pain in my heart when I was unable to name the anxiety I once felt. I felt overwhelmed and found it hard to decipher the panic I felt just in travelling in a moving vehicle or even watching them.

Loud noises and people speaking in loud tones disturbed me very deeply. It scattered my thoughts to hear loud noises and I was unable to pay heed to the thoughts that formed in my mind about the emotions that I was feeling.

For me, it was difficult to understand why I felt the way I dd and was looking for validation from all sources. It hurt me to see the difficulties surrounding my world.

When I got married into a family of four with a large group of relatives and deep social involvement, I was naturally overwhelmed and felt the pressure to perform under the pressure of the 'newly-wed bride' tag.

It was this pressure that increased the stress of performing and I felt anxious in a subtler way. I was exhilarated to be married as it was my long-standing dream. I was happy and excited. I was in a new phase of life. I felt accepted.

Along with this happiness came inevitable enthusiasm to become the 'perfect' daughter-in-law that I once knew I would become. I wished to sacrifice all my dreams and personal attachments just to be ideal.

The perception of 'ideal' woman in my eyes was influenced by the social expectations and norms. I was influenced by the way people perceived women. I was carried away and tried to overperform each time. All my attempts fell face first as the level of acceptance from the other involved parties is never the same as you wish it to be.

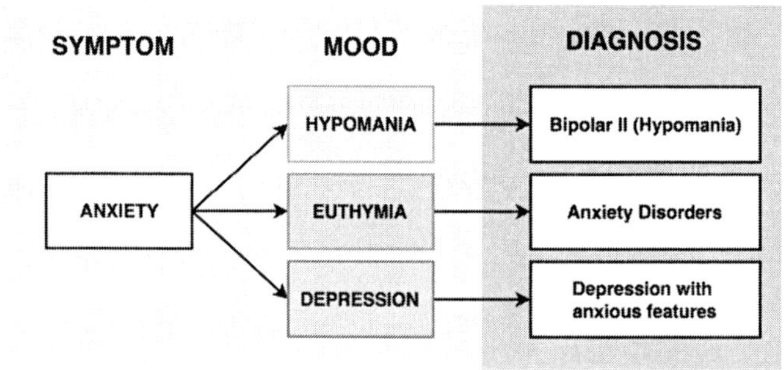

I was in a hurry to have a baby. I conceived within 9 months of my wedding. I was elated, but scared. I was terrified that my baby would be too fragile for the harsh, harsh world. I began to worry about the most precious and sacred life forming in my womb.

I was concerned beyond the limit. I developed extreme anxiety after having my baby. I was shivering through the process and was too scared to take my baby out of the postoperative ward.

I did not wish to leave the hospital. The drive home from the hospital was the most terrifying.

I did not wish to leave the controlled atmosphere of the hospital and did not wish to go anywhere. I felt like I needed the vigilance of the nurses.

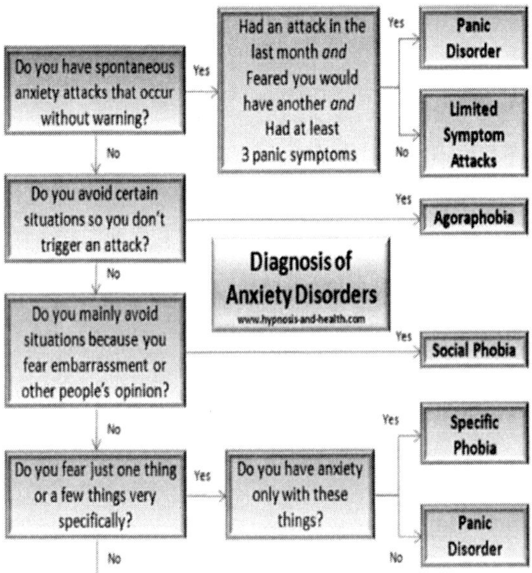

Source: https://www.hypnosis-and-health.com/

Up to two years of my baby's infancy, I struggled through inexplicable anguish and panic.

My husband was the constant listener of all my difficult emotions and I told him of the things that worried me. He took me to a psychiatrist and I was diagnosed with severe depression and anxiety.

I spoke my heart out and released all the pent-up emotions. I was given antidepressants and medication for anxiety. Simply listening to the physiological implications that have resulted in my anxiety and listen to the doctor tell me something apart from 'be strong' and 'do not be too sensitive' was a refreshing, welcome change.

I was happy and peaceful for the first time in years once I started the medication. I was able to sit in a car. I was able to sit in a bus with loud music. I was able to feel 'normal' and 'ordinary'.

I was able to go to office and not feel paranoid that people were mocking me. I was able to live. Again. Thanks to the diagnosis and treatment.

I felt alive again. I joined SBET institutions as faculty. I was back to teaching. I began to enjoy teaching and was ever so elated to feel normal again and was able to face my students.

I am happy to feel human again. I am elated to be able to feel normal like most people and get rid of my anxiety, depression, and paranoia. Medicine manages anxiety.

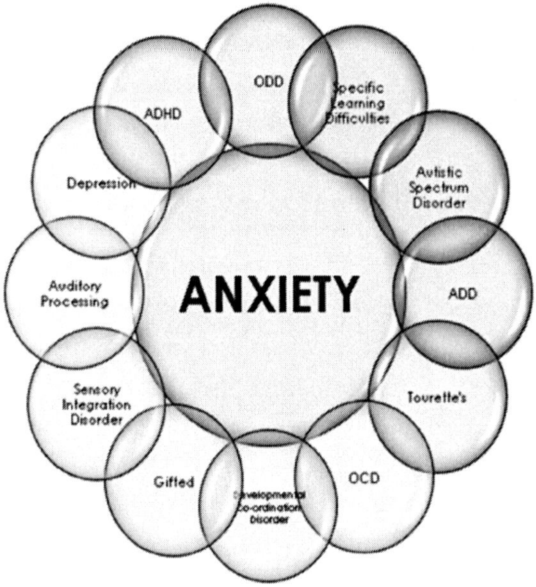

Source: https://www.lanc.org.uk/

It does not completely be done away with. It is a condition that needs to be managed. Anxiety leads to different conditions that are all connected to the central syndrome.

I have experienced phobia of loud noises and moving cars. The visuals of unwarranted catastrophes have disturbed me deeply. I have various visions of possible catastrophes rupturing my daily thoughts and emotions.

I have felt rushed and unbearably pushed to the edge. It is the most annoying thing in the world to know what you are going through but not being able to move the actual mountains. I have felt paralyzed in spirit as I have been unable to nurture the thoughts that poised me to the occasion.

Anxiety has its own way of making its way into your world and causing immense stress. The future seems abysmal and lifeless. I have forever been unable to gain perspective of my future and see it with brightness.

However, I was always moved by the diagnostic experience and the feeling of being understood. I felt peace after the longest time and felt validated in the true sense.

The reassurance was surreal and felt most refreshing. I could sleep peacefully after the longest time. I felt assured that there was an understanding of my condition and more people experienced it in the world.

The refreshing sense of diagnosis and treatment and the understanding of the different phobias makes one more compassionate about self. I was able to empathize with myself and be able to refresh my thoughts and emotions in the most valid way in ages. Life has a way of telling you that you are in the right hands once you learn to empathize with yourself. You feel like the emotions are all valid and real and you experience your own truth in the terms that make the most sense to you.

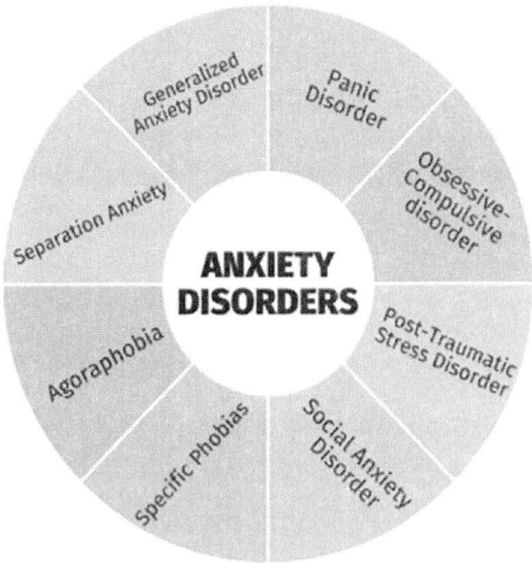

Source: https://buddyhelp.org/

I enjoyed the silence in the night where I was able to drift off to sleep once I took the tablets. The medication soothed my mind and I was able to sit quietly amidst chaos. I did not feel judged and I felt more human.

The experience of feeling like a normal human being and the feeling of belongingness is the most important validation that a person with anxiety requires. It is the most self-assuring journey. It makes you feel like your most genuine self.

I have been able to drift into the silences of the most genuine experience. I have been able to trace the reality of my experience into the self-functionality. My thoughts and emotions have felt justified and my heart, healed.

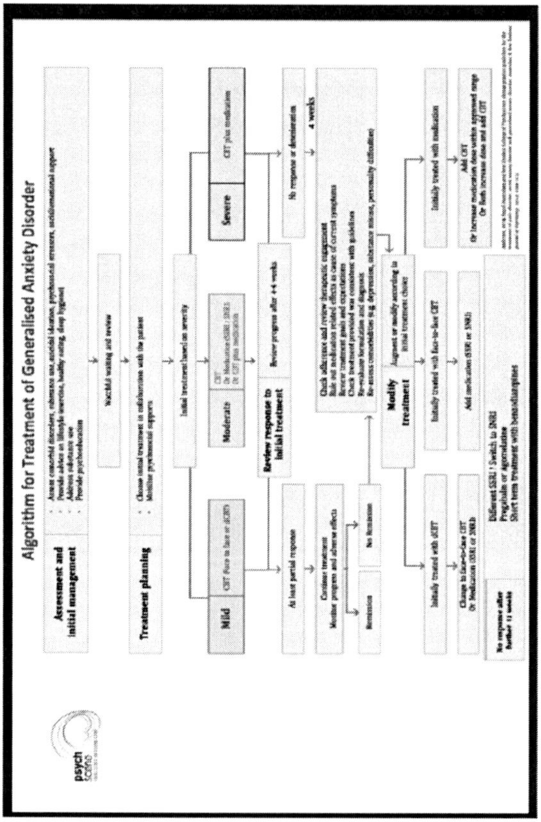

source:https://psychscenehub.com/

The phobia was immense. The cure, more natural than I had experienced it to be. The realness of the justification that is false and the method of treatment for generalized anxiety disorder is, in itself, real and satisfying.

I was given mild dosages. The initial response was noticeably positive. Thus, the dosage was validated and I felt like myself in a long time.

7. Complexity of the Mind

The mind is most complex. I have experienced difficult emotions with the elasticity immense pressure. It is unreal how the mind manifests such emotions without waiting for the response. It is the most magnetic thing in the world to experience such emotions with unmatched intensity.

I have often wondered how it is possible to feel lonely and disturbed in company altogether. I have often felt alone but felt alienated in company. I have experienced stress in the company of people, feeling judged and isolated. I have wished to make friends, but isolated myself from people. The paradoxical attitude of the mind is simply unreal.

How one accomplishes the experience is unjust, unfair, and unmediated. The stillness in silence is intoxicating and the sadness simply grows on you. You experience peace in loneliness and self-pity and do not wish to emerge from it.

You want to feel stuck in the emotions of life and be captivated in the self-destructing loop of faith. It is surreal and expansive. It is unnatural to feel silence so deeply. Or is it?

The leap of faith is intense and natural. It is all-consuming and fills in one a sense of satisfaction. It is far from despair that is felt in the loops of methodology that are used for the destruction of reality that shapes the ideas of success.

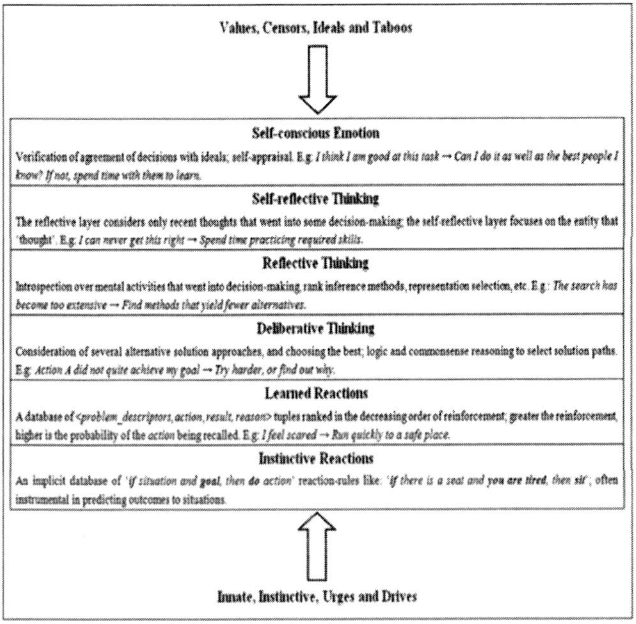

Citation: Banerjee and Pal, 2015

Why the mind complicates life is indistinct. The urge to feel all emotions deeply is unrecognizable. The reason for life's complexity is intense and distracting. Reason is intense and makes life more complex than ever.

It is not possible to make the most of the seasons that come and go. They change in events that gratify the soul. They make it more indulgent and make it a new beginning. These beginnings are emergent in their own ways. They make themselves available to the grace that consumes itself.

I have known the emotions that make me full. They make me feel more complete than can be. I am most gratified in the self-respecting loop of faith. I am more than grateful for the life that was handed down to me. The birth of my son was the most gratifying experience.

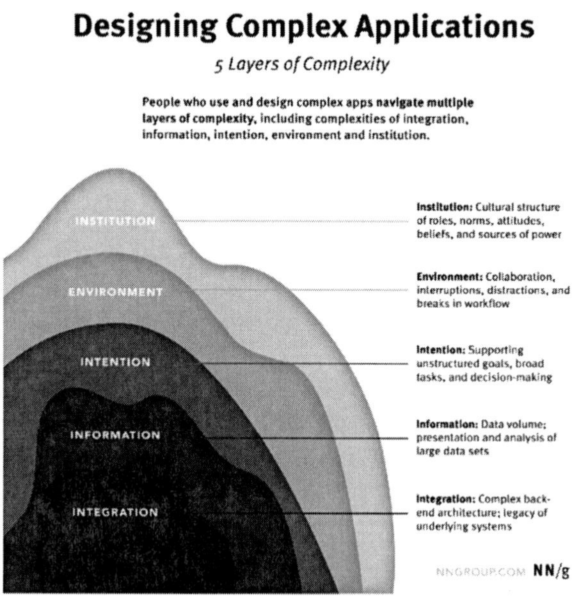

Source: https://www.nngroup.com/

My pain turned into pleasure and I was at my emotional highest as I held him in my arms. His presence in my arms and his soft breath made me fall in love immensely and unconditionally and experience the divine vision of God himself. I remember looking into his pitch-black eyes and seeing the entire universe. I was stunned, spellbound, and ecstatic. I love Him.

My son is God to me. He is the vision of God that I was able to fall in love with his grace. He filled my heart. But made me anxious, too. He made me feel his divine presence in my life. However, I was worried that the world would hurt him. It killed me. This anxiety.

The reassurance of love that my son gave in my heart is surreal and exhilarant. I experienced the highest dose of anxiety, fearing that I would drop him from the stairs or choke him on my breastmilk.

These thoughts are hurtful even to reminisce. They kill me while I write them too. I lived with such unspoken anxiety, panic, and fear. I was unable to feel the presence of the positive waves in my life. They were mired in the panic-stricken thoughts that filled my heart.

They increased in intensity each time I looked at life from a different perspective. I felt indulged in the thought of love and loss. I was entangled in the thoughts that pressed against my heart.

These thoughts not only disturb you, they also change the entire game of existence. They make one feel out of touch with themselves. They are unable to feel the pleasure of unspoken thoughts that complete an individual.

They are all the same. These thoughts. They complete you, yet make you feel incomplete. They change the way you think. They change your destiny.

Source: https://eocinstitute.org/

The conscious and unconscious mind form the layers of the mind. They coordinate in making space for the various thoughts that you have as they make the world go in circles and make you feel stuck due to their repetitive patterns.

Fears of the subconscious mind give no space to think. They make you wonder if what you thought was even real. They confuse and disperse your ideas of faith.

In times like these, my firm faith and belief in God has uplifted me. My son's presence was proof enough that God exists in my life. I have a firm belief that God will take care of me. I believe that I will never be too ruined for Him to not be able to revive me.

My faith in the divine feminine, Goddess *Chamundi* has kept me alive. She has guided me, soothed me, made me sleep in her lap. Her flowing hair and the flavor of vermillion has purified my soul. The purity of her presence in my vicinity has felt irreplaceable.

The thoughts of wondering that she understands me and stands by me is immensely wonderful. The feeling of her being in my presence and make me understand her everlasting stature is unreal and surreal.

The experience is divine. She holds my fingers and takes me through the fields. Sometimes blindfolded, sometimes aware. The consciousness that holds her grace and the subconscious that holds her dreams both play a very crucial role in understanding her inevitable faith.

The occurrences of life feel like they are happening at me and they make one feel the sense of being a victim of situations.

It is most stressful and they hinder the process of healing as they are give higher power to imagination.

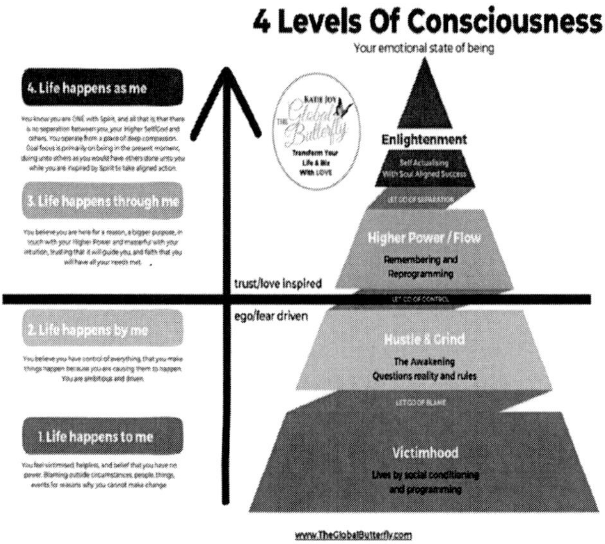

https://www.theglobalbutterfly.com/

The mind is a complex puzzle. It is a maze. It takes you through mind's fields holding hands like a soulmate. It is most complex as it is layered. It is the most intense experience to understate its fears and the imagination that lights up its very being.

It houses doubts and fears. It makes for the most complex struggle. They make love to fear and bear the lovechild of wildflowers in the mind. These thoughts are unruly. They are unethical and adulterated.

They make the most of the dark places in your head and they try to utilize them against your will. I have come out of such emotions solely through the faith in Her that has uplifted me and made me emerge above the psyche of the subconscious.

The personality that shapes you into the being that you wish to be is the physical world that makes you believe in the self-conscious realms of truth.

You become aware of the most conscious life's puzzles and make the most of the ego that tells you that everything in the world is real. It feels more internal and personally unconscious thoughts are interpreted in the devotion that holds the complexes of the shadowed thoughts.

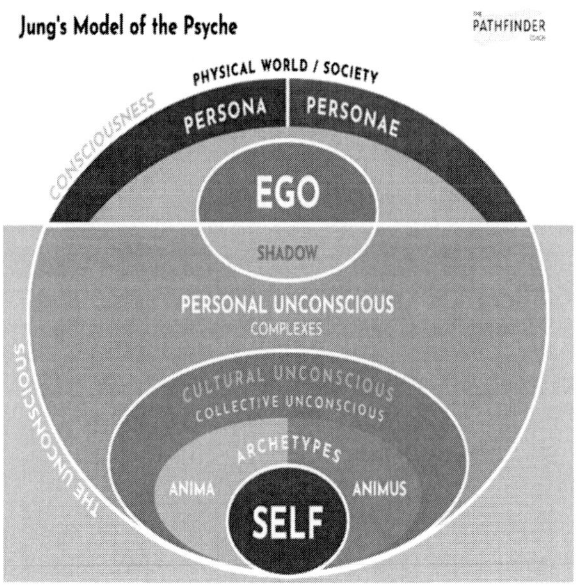

Source: https://thepathfinder.org/

The model of the conscious mind tells one that the subtlety of emotions may be rewarded in their very being. They are self-replicating and they make way for the balance of the mind.

These thoughts understate the emergence of the truths that spill the nectar of goodness. They fulfill the desires that make for the most repetitive patterns.

They fulfill the love that spills out of the bags of truth. The cat finally escapes the bag. The truth finally comes out. They make you realize the penchant that the mind has for complicating the thoughts that fill your heart.

They make the most stupendous self-conscious images that shape the mentality of grace. They are unrealistic and make the most beautiful pictures in the heart. They make them come through to me in times when I need them most.

I have dreamed of having a tempestuous affair with time. The time that rules everything. I have dreamed of attaining God. I have made peace with life on its own terms.

The love for faith makes the world go around. They make the genuine desire to be real and raw. They make you feel vulnerable and broken in ways you do not realize are real.

They are stray emotions that hold value in the heart. They are personal and real. They are small and big. They are oxymorons.

8. Stress, Depression, and Anxiety – A Personal Experience

Stress, depression, and anxiety are all experiences that do not let life pass into expected results. When I was a child, I felt like doing my homework and attending school were extremely stressful, not from the perspective of learning or academic strife but being in the company of peers who felt like enemies.

Not because I treated them so, but because they treated me like that. There was a time I was falsely accused of stealing a classmate's book just being blamed as I was the quietest child in class.

I have drowned in self-pity and not been able to retain the peace that I found at home. I have been mocked as being too slow. And yes, I was slow. I felt like I would hurt somebody's feelings if I spoke too loudly. I was, thus, inaudible.

I felt like I would hurt things around me if I touched them too hard. Thus, I was too weak. Too slow, too soft, too weak for the world.

I was depressed. I had a terrible experience. I was in seventh grade. A boy in my class who sat behind me, groped me. Touched me very, *very* inappropriately on the pretext of looking at my badge. I was scandalized, hurt, and disgusted.

I felt like the world ended for me. I did not have the courage to talk about it. I did not have the courage to tell anybody and report his behavior. I remember I cried a river and felt filthy. I felt like I did not wish to go back to school.

After weeks, I told my mother. I remember feeling like a huge boulder was lifted off my chest. It was so obvious and so sudden. I begged her to not report it as I wanted to save myself embarrassment.

He did not repeat it. I was afraid of him. I was disgusted with him. I despised him. I still do. I was too scared to talk to boys. I do not know why. I was unable to make friends with them naturally. Perhaps because I felt I was too feminine for them to understand me.

I felt like my world was entirely different from theirs. I felt like the girls did not understand my world either. Perhaps I was too dreamy and too far fetched from all of them. I had no friends.

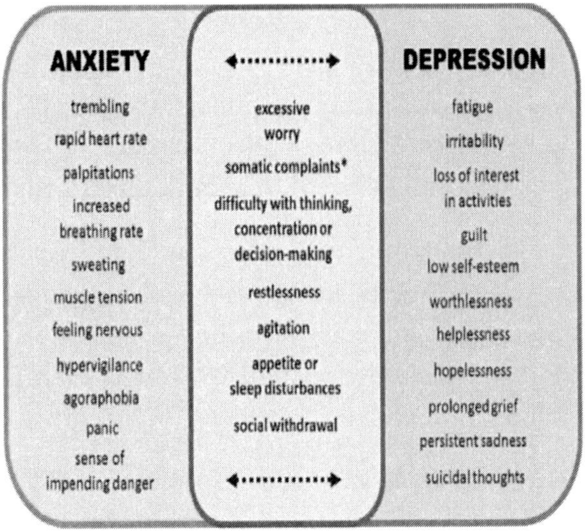

source: https://lindamagsoncounselling.com.au/

As the figure above illustrates, anxiety and depression both vary in their own selves. They harness a similarity and an intersection with their shared symptoms.

The withdrawal from social circles is a real problem.

I grew into a teenager. I was mocked in college. There were boys I was silently attracted to. I was too scared to admit it. I felt like I was too ugly for them to notice. Again, I could not make friends with anybody.

I could not find girls who shared my ideas in life. I could not talk to boys. I was too stressed by the academic part of my college life. I felt left behind and felt like I could not cope. I was too afraid to face my lectures for no fault of mine.

I was the most peculiar student. At least, that was how I felt. I felt too different and thought that my fellow students mocked me. I felt too alone. I had a select few friends. I wished to escape the stress and so I opted out of my classes.

I went home and sat alone, wishing to have more friends. I constantly felt stressed. The words in my book floated past my eyes. I could not grasp them. I was always a 'good' student. However, I was unable to retain that in the pre-university phase.

I could not learn what was expected of me. I remember being good at languages and biology. I was unable to concentrate on subjects that I did not connect with emotionally.

I had a bad experience in college. One of my lecturers randomly read the writings on my t-shirt. I felt mocked and ridiculed. My mother said it was because I wore the shirt that I had the embarrassing experience. I could have worn something more decent.

My complaints were silent. I felt like I was blamed for something that was not my fault. I was alone. I was deaf to my own complaints. I cried. In heaps. It was then that I realized life was very fragile. I was walking to the bus stop. Truck loaders passed insensitive and vulgar remarks. I remember their words even today.

I still feel overwhelmed when I remember those words. The disturbance causes anxiety and shame. Is it true for everyone or those with anxiety? I wonder.

I was afraid of life. I was unable to go further than my perceived reality. I could not make friends as I felt they all laughed at me and that I was too peculiar for them. I felt too different from their lives and could not identify with any one of them.

I was depressed and anxious. I could not study.

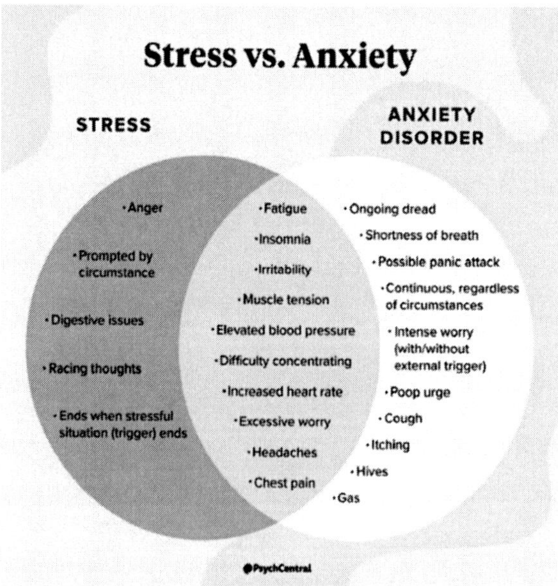

Source: https://psychcentral.com/

The figure shows the symptoms of anxiety and stress and how they share them. I have experienced all of the above symptoms and felt too lonely and unable to handle all that life sent towards me.

I went on to do my engineering degree. I had the best educational experience there. I met a couple of girls who I felt were similar in their interest in studies. I kept my personal emotions at bay. I was truly passionate about the subject that I had picked up.

I loved to study biotechnology. I enjoyed the laboratory experiments. However, I felt like I would make mistakes and was unable to focus. I was stressed about not being able to do the experiments right. I was always stressed. However, I did well academically.

I felt like I was winning at life. I was getting my degree in engineering. I studied a great deal. I truly enjoyed studying. I felt normal as I had friends and was happy to be a part of the institution.

I learned a great number of things in my college and also performed well. There was a sense of satisfaction within me. I was anxious to perform well but was quite happy with myself.

I was able to feel happy after a long time. I was able to remind myself that life is happy and satisfying. It was a wonderful time to be satisfied with life and be in a position to feel satisfied with life all over again.

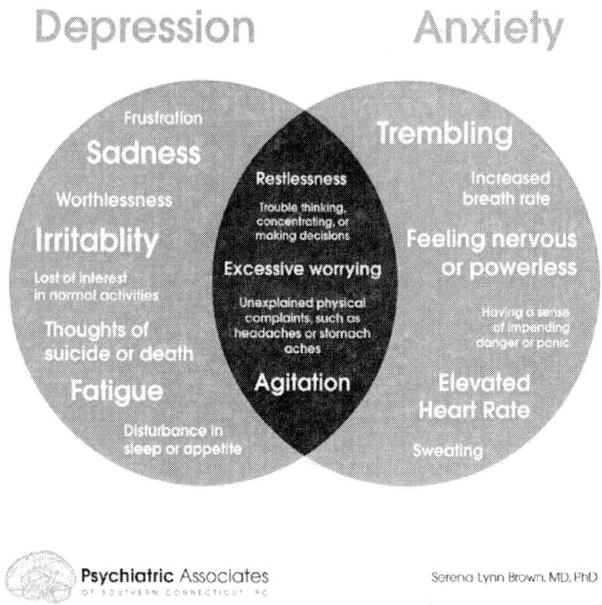

Source: https://www.ctpsychtms.com/

I then pursued my masters in the United Kingdom. There, I felt rejuvenated and felt like I met the people that I could truly connect with. However, in the background, stress remained and so did depression and anxiety.

Although, I must admit, they were far less in expression. The expressions of frustration, sadness, irritability and worthlessness were far less than usual. As I felt quite accomplished. I did feel bouts of depression and worrying, restlessness, and agitation.

I felt lonely and sad when I was alone. I was terrified of loneliness. I had trouble thinking and making decisions. I experienced racism and, in those moments, I felt like complaining to God.

I was tired and exhausted and felt overwhelmed when I had to face people and examinations. I performed well academically. I even bagged a good project.

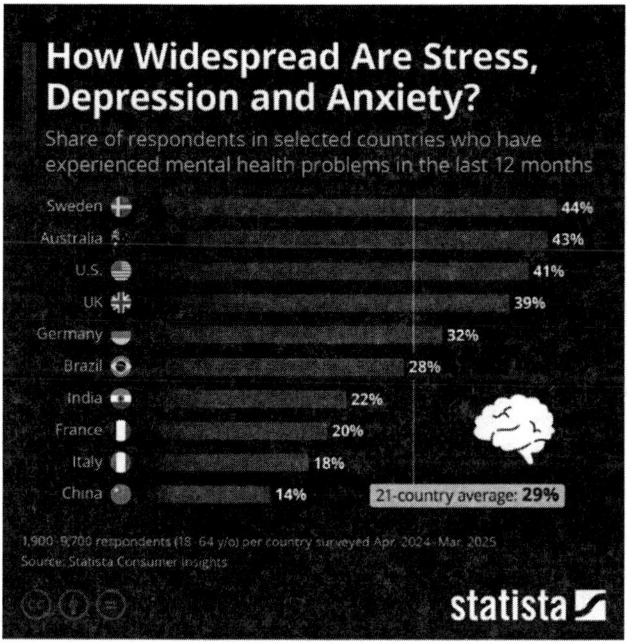

Source: https://www.statista.com/

I was able to make very good friends who I identified with and who did not judge me. However, I wished for validation, even then. From most people. I wanted to feel alive. I needed to feel desirable and wanted.

I believe in statistics that say that anxiety and depression are widespread. However, I felt most times like I was alone and was the only one experiencing the things I was going through.

I returned to India. I felt judged and out of place. I felt like I was back home. I felt lonely and isolated. I wished to go back. I was desperate to go back to the UK. I missed my life there terribly.

I felt completely displaced and depressed. I was susceptible to the sadness that came with being displaced. I was completely stressed and was unable to find ground with reality.

I felt like I could not find a job. I felt like I had disappointed my father. I felt inferior to my peers. I felt like I could never do enough to be good enough. For him. For them. I then got into teaching. I loved my job. I loved teaching. I thrived in the college where I had a special relationship with my students.

I then switched jobs ever so frequently. I could not stick to jobs as I felt like everybody hated me. I was paranoid. I could not stay in any job more than a few months.

I was unable to understand the process of stability.

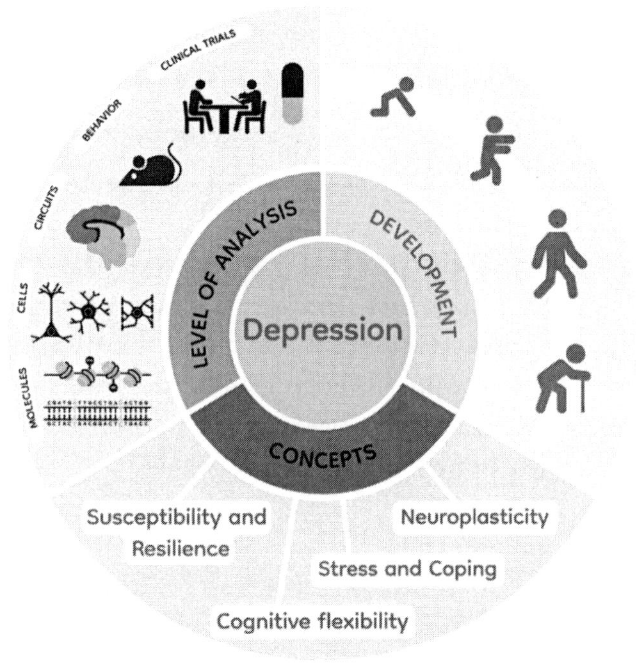

Citation: Akil and Nestler, 2023

Marriage

My wedding was a whirlwind of an event. It was both surreal and enchanting. The proposal came out of the blue and once I met my now husband for the first time, I felt the peace I was seeking for all these years had presented itself to me in the form of a person.

We chatted for a half hour and his refreshingly mature perspectives on life made me feel peace like never before. Of course, I had to say yes. I was on cloud nine. But, as they say, disaster has a way of striking just when you settle into the warm rays of sunshine and the sky becomes overcast again.

A week before our engagement, my mother fell critically ill. I was disturbed beyond imagination and was pushed back into the darkness. But this time, I had an anchor who kept me from sinking – my husband. His words and his unwavering presence sailed me through. The anxiety that the wonderful dream of the wedding may break and as I lost most things just when they came to fruition, I would lose him to some other girl, obviously much prettier and more fortunate than me engulfed me. I drowned in that anxiety and sought his reassurance a million times. And he reassured me – Every. Single. Time.

The marriage was a mixed bag. An insufferable introvert like me was put into an orthodox, large family with hundreds of relatives. People would come home and stay for days. I had to sleep amidst so many people. I had to participate in household chores. Strangely, I was over-enthusiastic to become the ideal 'housewife'. The most orthodox version of me came into being – seamlessly. I found myself sitting on the floor and eating with all those people chatting with them like they were my own. And perhaps, they were.

However, I was over-enthusiastic. I wanted to do everything that I possibly could. I was enthused and wanted to do all the household chores. When I was told off and refused the opportunity, when I was judged for being 'quiet' when I was talking the most I had in my entire life, when I received silent treatment for no apparent fault of mine, my heart broke. I wanted my mother. I cried in silence. For days.

You get used to new things and life teaches you that not everything is as bad as you perceive it. You learn that you have limitations and you mustn't go into realms that do not belong to you.

I learned this lesson a tad bit late. Now four years into our marriage, I have struck the right chord (with the help of my husband, of course), and now I have the most supportive family and have formed a warm bond with them all.

9. Does it Leave for Good?

The most pertinent question that haunts those plagued by anxiety is if it will ever leave, and for good? However, this remains unanswered. The closest I have come to answering this question is that it requires perennial management and learning to live without medication.

My wavering mind constantly battled the ups and downs of living in solitude. I have often been reminded of the solitary life in deep vigilance of love and its longing. I have forever longed for a peaceful place to rest and love that felt like home.

My anxiety has deeply deprived me of stabilizing emotions, always keeping me vigilant and under pressure to be and exist. My existence has been a challenge to me due to its unflinching faith in resistance to endeavors of peace.

I have often envisioned my life with a peaceful and loving family wishing for lasting peace. I have attempted to put together the shredded bits of my heart to make a complete picture that colored my life in white – the hue of peace.

My life has stopped several times. Each time I experienced anxiety attacks, I have lost my heart to the sunburnt hues of orange and red that color the sky at every sunrise and sunset. I have been upset with the sun for not rising in my life.

I have felt like I am left behind by life and running late for my train and even missing it. I have waited on random platforms for trains of life to pause for me and lost count of those that rushed past ignoring my existence altogether. I have felt forgotten and watched seasons zap past without acknowledging my presence.

Such was the forging of love and loss in my life where I have never been involved in performing the act of acquitting peaceful existence apart from love's betrayal of time.

Life gave me options to leave behind the ruins of my detached mind. Was I detached even? Perhaps distant, but not completely detached. I have been attached to life in its fullest form and been snatched away from its pace.

I have lived in a rush and sometimes in pointless pauses. I was deprived of solace while anxiety, in all its audacity, pushed me to believe there was no life apart from death.

I have been given the restless regards of sleepless nights that taught me to remember and not forget those important times when I lost all those things that I prayed for. I was handed the depression of not being able to rise from its clutches and separate myself from the shackles of disillusionment.

The desperation to find peace is inevitable and real. It takes you through the pages of nostalgia and wishes to return to childhood. To flip through pages of children's books and pretend to outlive the nasty experiences that dictate the spell of life.

The level of understanding that dictates this process is true regardless of the situation. I have been reminded of the process of the transformation that allows one to keep up with life. I have tended to neglect my self-care and become completely drowned in depression where I have struggled to keep myself alive.

I never had the urge to take care of myself or dress for occasions as I found them entirely pointless and nasty.

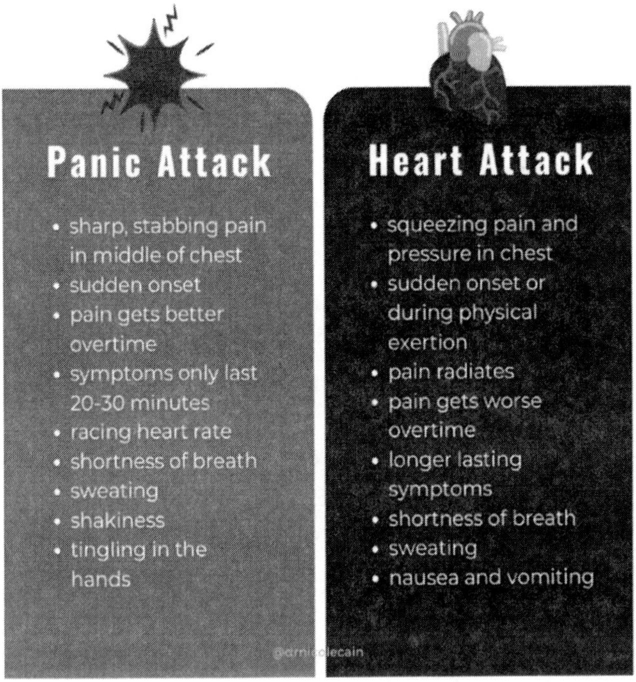

Source: https://drnicolecain.com/

The glaring reality of life while panic attacks dictate your existence is intrusive and pulls you into a vicious loop that repeats itself in episodes when life passes by in a blur.

It is alarming how closely panic attacks resemble heart attacks. The sharp, stabbing pain in the chest causes increased anxiety and depression. It is in the middle of the chest as described in the list above.

Heart attacks, they say pose a squeezing, excruciating pain in the chest with a sense of pressure. The physical pain alleviates itself over time. The heart attack is sudden and has an onset with physical exertion. I have experienced subtle shocks in the tips of my fingers and numbing of the brain.

I have also experienced balance issues and felt like I would faint in a heap. The subtle reality of life is so consuming that it does not relent itself in the least. I have experienced severe nausea and also thrown up to elevate my pain.

The attacks have lasted as long as 30 minutes and the palpation in my thumping chest was so intense that I feared others would hear it beating.

I have experienced sweat breakouts and immense depression. I have experienced subtle shocks at the tips of my fingers. I have wished I could simply die.

In response to stress, the body releases the stress hormone. It eventually affects the organs of the body, impairing their functionality as illustrated in the figure. It is difficult to manage such anxiety.

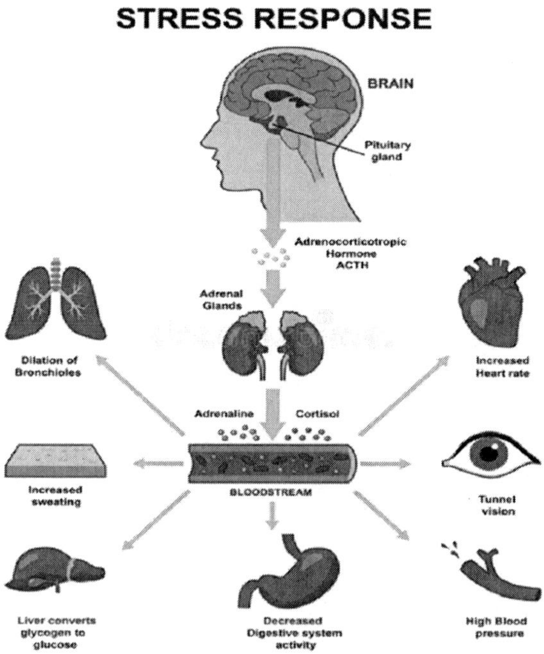

Source: https://www.dreamstime.com/

It is worse to assume that life will go on like it should without worrying about anxiety. It leaves you no choice. It forces you to think about it and manage it as it is the most driven point of your thought.

It is the most engaging thought and the most disturbing reality of the mind. It confuses reality with its own fertile imagination and catastrophizes all situations. For me workplace was threatening and so was home, so was the world.

I figured leaving the world as the only probable solution to life's challenges. Mostly challenges of dealing with the anxious mind. I never felt like leaving temples. I wished to live inside the premises of a temple, envying the women married to priests who get to live in the premises and sweep the floors of the temple. I have wished I could be them.

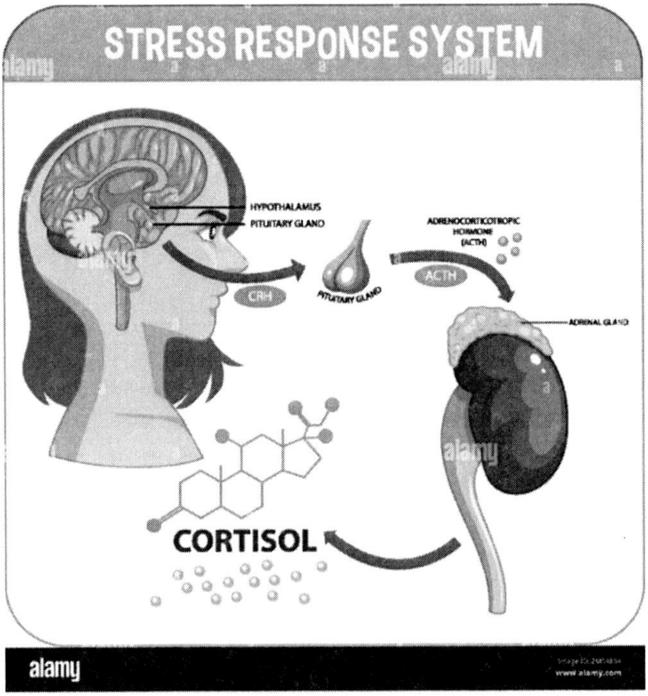

Source: www.alamy.com

It does leave – temporarily. It comes back again, and again, and again. It is impossible to get rid of anxiety. One only learns to manage it. Eventually, the heart accepts this truth. However, it is the biggest conjecture of truth and reality that confuse the mind. They delve even deeper into the stress response. I remember working relentlessly without even wanting a break for lunch. I have always experienced escapism.

The activation of the stress system

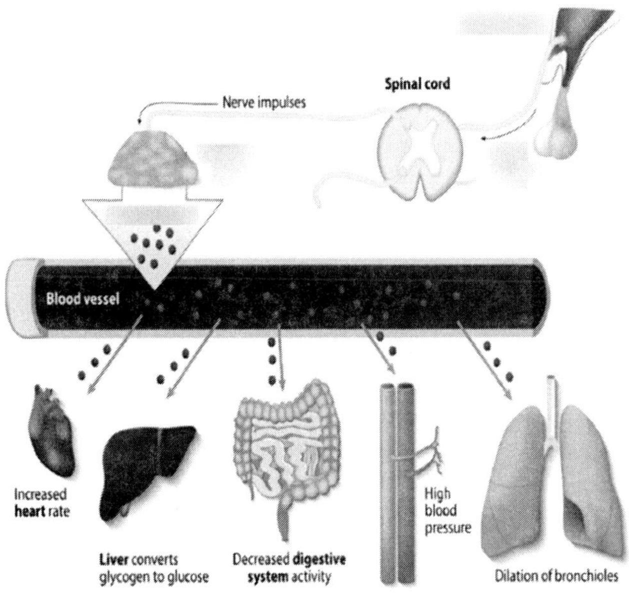

Source: www.quizlet.com

Escapism never helps the alleviation process. It only convices the mind to let go of temporary expectations. It convinces the mind that nothing good can happen in one's life. I remember feeling a deep sense of envy towards fictitious characters in television dramas and movie scripts.

This was almost a mockery of reality. It was as if I was convinced that reality was far more contextual than imagination. I was drowned in imaginary thoughts indulging them and feeling desperate for validation.

10. Panic and Anxiety – Understanding the Intersection

The intersection between panic disorder and anxiety are questionable and horrifying to the lay person. As somebody who has been experiencing both, the difference is unintelligible and blur.

Panic attacks happen at the most unlikely times and they plaque the innocent mind to an uncanny extent. They cause physical implications such as sweating, formation of a lump in the throat and increased heart rate.

The pulse races as if clutching for life and demands immediate attention and tender and soothing care. It is impossible to resist such thoughts and make way for more positive and peaceful ones. Panic convinces the mind that something is terribly wrong and needs to be taken care of with immediate attention.

I have dealt with such perceived urgency, fighting for truth and relying solely on the perpetrated perceptions of fading reality.

The response to stressful or feared situations almost always results in panic. I always feared moving vehicles and loud noises. Travelling with loud music and people chattering was the biggest nightmare for me. I almost felt like people in the car have conspired against me and my fear and are talking in their loudest tones just to mock me.

Such paranoia resulted in more chaotic emotions and borderline hatred and increased fear for the situation. Again, I have resorted to avoidance and felt like running away from the situation. I almost felt like getting off the car and walking in the most silent corners of the road without the fear of catastrophes occurring with the car I was travelling in just to avoid the situation altogether.

The attacks lasted for long durations and interfered with my every day activities to an extent that I felt the only solution was to avoid life completely. Such thoughts can be both alarming and soothing. It is this intersection that is confusing to the fresh mind as it fears abandonment.

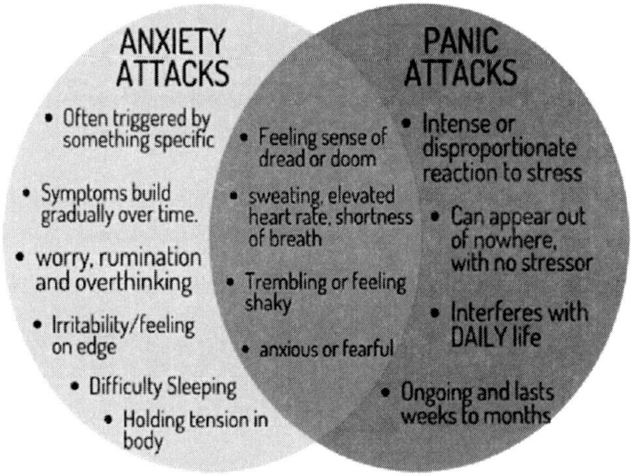

Source: https://narodnatribuna.info/

The mind races between the chaos and reaches points of ultimate survival.

The intersection between anxiety and panic is a close juncture and actually conjoins each other in an octet of symptoms. The body reacts to such thoughts and fears and it is no longer a fleeting emotion that dies if not fed.

The urge to 'rest in peace' forever is a functional distress that results from daily activities. Such perceived urgency is a distance that is created between the mind and reality. It steers into the classical mode of function that mind their ways into everyday life.

Stressful events and situations result in modes of no contact with reality switching their positions ever so often. I have found solace in the most random places waiting for peace to set in and stay. I am unable to process the connection between the reality of thoughts and anxiety.

I have been unable to travel in buses, in cars or even sit by in the balcony watching a vehicle speed by and praying relentlessly that catastrophes and accidents must not occur. I have visualized the world going to pieces and shreds with remarkable blasts and boom resulting in doom.

Such doom is the expected end and something that disturbed me deeply. I watched enormous festive lights on the streets and visualized the large amount of electricity that they leverage and how there could be potential environmental abuse and ultimate crisis and catastrophe.

The intersection between anxiety and panic as suggested in the picture above is the real distinction between the two. I have lost sleep trying to gather my thoughts and regain the consciousness of the reality. However, it is most difficult to understand the depths of these emotions and be able to find the peace in the resulting chaos and tempestuous emotions.

I have often feared the world and felt like I have been going in loops and circles of never-ending viciousness. I often feared how to belong and remain calm in situations that were taxing to the mind. It is difficult to wrap one's head around these challenging emotions and be able to understand the gravity or their intensity.

I have felt most challenged and devastated in times when these emotions have overpowered me with their convincing ideas of catastrophe. How does one deal with such spiteful emotions? It almost feels like the mind is playing against itself.

The heart feels heavy and satirizes the gravitas of reality that is crushed by the thoughts that anxiously fill the mind and relentlessly grab one's shoulders and shake up the spirits of animated mindlessness.

The onset of panic attacks is sudden and can reduce in a matter of minutes. However, anxiety attacks are more intense and prolonged. The physiological symptoms of panic attack and the emulate the symptoms of a cardiac arrest. The situational anxiety and panic are extremely real.

It feels overwhelming to experience a panic attack. I feel most intimidated while facing such issues. I feel devastated, breathless, and magnetically drawn towards death as the ultimate and final solution. Panic attacks are sudden and merciless. It feels unreal to experience them and feel the rapid heartbeat and nausea episodes increase the intensity of the episode.

I have experienced extreme giddiness and fatigue that nearly killed me in the end. The trigger factor for such panic attacks was not discernable. It was always most difficult to handle such attacks. In both cases, there is the experience of pain in the chest and shortness of breath.

I have felt intimidated and crushed in the episodes of panic as it washed away the truths of life and mired them in depressive anxiety. These episodic trials have vested my inheritance of anxiety perhaps through familial chains.

I have felt shackled in the rapid beating of my heart and caused my breathing to stop. These pauses in breath and the whirling decisions of my dizzy mind all intertwined to form the discomforting situational agony.

The anguish of not being able to control my emotions and the feeling of being unwell all form a triggered response which cause attacks of anxiety. These are typically short in duration and trigger the fear of death and catastrophic events.

It is quite opposite to anxiety attacks which are long drawn and specifically prolonged and they cause similar symptoms and are less intense than panic attacks. They do not jab your heart with the same pain but keep convincing you that life is not as fair and simple as you wish it to be.

This leads to weeks and months of symptomatic uneasiness which are opposite to the intense and episodic panic attacks.

Source: https://www.ar15.com/

The stimuli of shortness of breath and causative chest pain which are all apparent reasons for difficulty in breathing. The panic attacks are all an advanced strategic pause that can conceive the idea of loss.

I believe I was perhaps vulnerable to the panic disorder due to genetic factors even. I feel certain that I was exposed to homeostatic triggers due to certain genetic predisposition. This has led to chronic illnesses including regurgitation (GERD) and digestive disorders that have had long-term implications.

Such chronic illnesses have affected my way of life and made my happiness feel endangered with a sharp pointed edge hanging over my head in a constant and persevering attempt to kill. As they say, "*what doesn't kill you, makes you stronger*", it does indeed make one stronger and more capable of dealing with what life hands you down.

However, I have been baffled at the endless possibilities of untruths spoken by my anxiety and sewn into the grudgingly rough fabric of panic-laden paths that lead into the well of dark, dark silence.

Panic feels like a constant burden and a response to threat. This system of response in both organic and sporadic. It makes an uncanny connection with the body causing hyperventilation, and an exaggerated cardiovascular response.

The response is contextual and it causes excruciating pain in the heart. What the above figure suggests as anticipatory anxiety is the anxiety that comes with anticipating danger.

The cycle of panic and anxiety include triggers which are correlated to perceived threats and anticipation of danger. The anxiety and depression go together and form loops of catastrophising and misinterpretation.

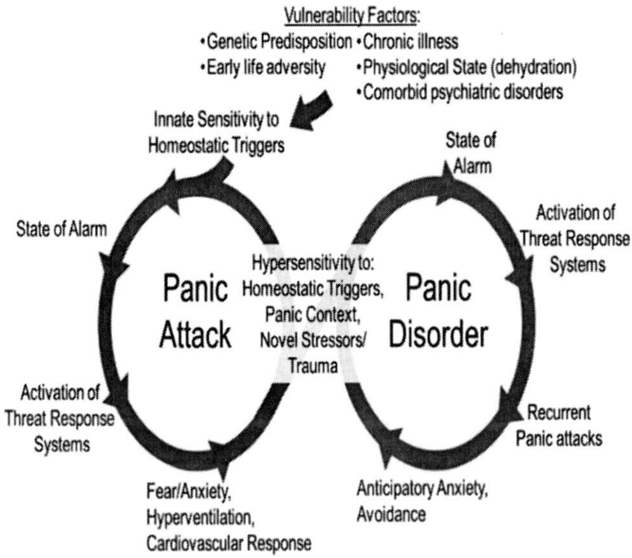

Source: https://www.frontiersin.org/

There are several physiological symptoms that lead to misinterpretation of the situation and perceive dangers in normal situations. This leads to systematic avoidance of life in general. Such catastrophic thoughts are assimilated into the process of catastrophizing.

Normal situations are transformed into triggers of anxiety and panic which cause avoidance of life and all ordinary situations and cause a cyclical imprisonment in one's own thoughts and emotions.

Such anxiety is ridiculously taxing as it causes depression in its most organic form and puts away thoughts of panic into boxes that are full of inadvertent ideas and meltdowns.

It is important though that such thoughts persevere into responses that are sporadic and organically divided into positives and negatives.

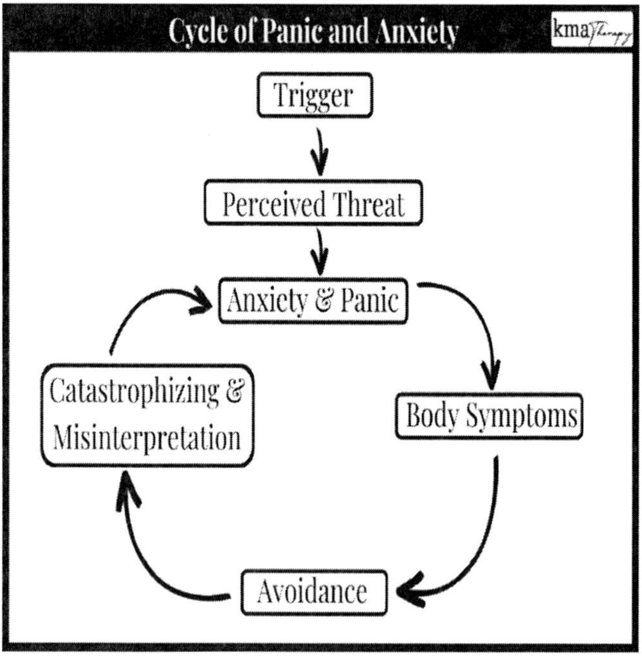

Source: https://www.kmatherapy.com/

As the above figure suggests, the cycle of anxiety and panic form loops that are never-ending and fear avoidant behaviours. They are constant reminders of faith.

Hypervigilance is a symptom caused by physical sensations or images thoughts and situations are all perceived threats. The anxiety mounds in various forms that are all responses to stress.

My sensations and reactions indeed felt amplified and increased into the catastrophizing that results from ordinary situations. The various physical sensations include rapid heartbeat, pain in the chest, and difficulty in breathing.

It is accompanied by racing heart and relentless breathing that pounds in the heart. These thoughts are destructive and sabotage the well-being of the heart. I have voiced the illusions of my mind with the remainder of my mind.

It is an impossible belligerence that crosses the mind making it a chaotic possibility. Open to surrender, it mends the mind in regard to the ordinary truth. Such thoughts are captivating and magnetic in their presence. Seamless in their transition, they reverberate in resounding denials as life passes on carelessly.

I have watched my illusions through the window as seasons pass through like dawn to dusk, wondering in meaningful and rare silences that seep into the heart.

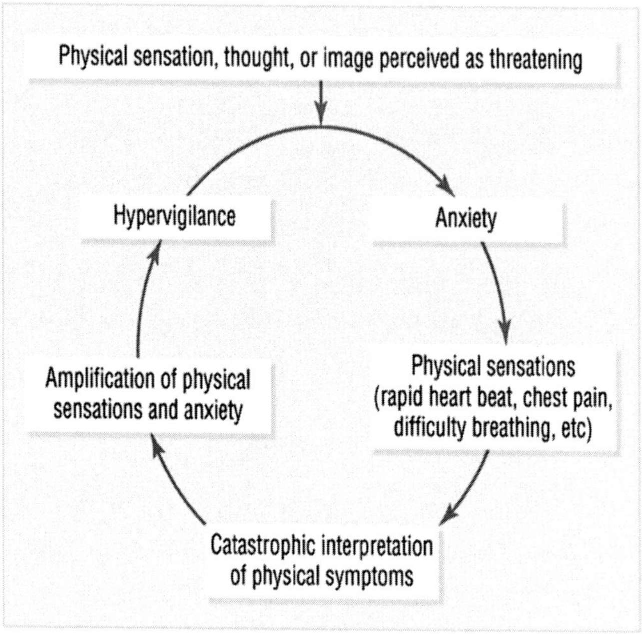

Citation: Taylor et al, 2006

The interpretations can be many but the reason – isolated. I have been warned through countless sources to be silent and vigilant as winds of anxiety whisper in unabashed persistence.

In all, I have survived the chasms of flames that burn from the interiors of the heart, charring the reality in soot that cannot be forever erased. To articulate my most dreaded fears and most sacred prayers and bind them together in a book is my sincerest effort to reach out to anybody that might be shackled in its dark embrace. I wish to tell you that there is a way out; what is also true is that it takes enormous effort to come out of the dark tunnel – and more so to remain outside of it.

Although I have not yet come into remission, I have come a long way into my journey and feel more normalcy in my life. This journey has both enriched me and warped me with its entanglements and warm embraces. There were times of depth that stirred my emotions, churned my feelings, and also deep silences that warmed my heart. I continue to manage my anxiety and live life with mindfulness. I send my prayers to all those souls that can relate to this sometimes frantic, sometimes forlorn search for elusive peace.

References

1.*American Psychological Association.* Available at: https://www.apa.org/topics/anxiety (Accessed: 07 November 2025).

2. (2020) *Review of maier et al* [Preprint]. doi:10.5194/tc-2020-185-rc2.

3. Wittchen, H., Hoyer, J. and Friis, R. (2001) 'Generalized anxiety disorder – a risk factor for depression?', *International Journal of Methods in Psychiatric Research,* 10(1), pp. 52–57. doi:10.1002/mpr.100.

4. Halbreich, U. (2003) 'Anxiety disorders in women: A developmental and Lifecycle Perspective', *Depression and Anxiety,* 17(3), pp. 107–110. doi:10.1002/da.10108.

5. *Female Hormones and Mental Health* (no date) *Link Between Hormones and Mental Health in Women.* Available at: https://www.hiranandanihospital.org/blog-details/link-between-hormones-and-mental-health-in-women (Accessed: 07 November 2025).

6. Gray, J.A. and McNaughton, N. (2024) *The neuropsychology of anxiety: An enquiry into the*

functions of the Septo-Hippocampal System. Oxford: Oxford University Press.

7.Sun, X. *et al.* (2023) 'Psychological birth trauma: A concept analysis', *Frontiers in Psychology*, 13. doi:10.3389/fpsyg.2022.1065612.

8.*Bhagavad-Gītā as it is 5.29.* Available at: https://vedabase.io/en/library/bg/5/29/ (Accessed: 08 November 2025).

9. Alsuhibani, Azzam & Shevlin, Mark & Freeman, Daniel & Sheaves, Bryony & Bentall, Richard. (2022). Why conspiracy theorists are not always paranoid: Conspiracy theories and paranoia form separate factors with distinct psychological predictors. PLOS ONE. 17. e0259053. 10.1371/journal.pone.0259053.

10. The neurobiology of stress: Vulnerability, resilience, and major depression Huda Akil https://orcid.org/0000-0003-0623-1056 akil@umich.edu and Eric J. Nestle

11. Taylor C B. Panic disorder *BMJ* 2006; 332 :951 doi:10.1136/bmj.332.7547.951